KNOW ME HERE

An Anthology of Poetry by Women

Edited with an Introduction by
Katherine Hastings

WordTemple Press
Santa Rosa, CA

Library of Congress Control Number: 2017946777

CONTENTS

Amulet for Women — Annie Finch   ix

Introduction   xi

Devreaux Baker   1
    Invocation for Spring
    We Show Each Other Our Scars
    Dancing at the Round House

Ellen Bass   6
    The Orange-and-White High-Heeled Shoes
    Reincarnation
    Taking Off the Front of the House

Elizabeth Bradfield   10
    Pursuit
    Dispatch from this Summer
    Repair

Janine Canan   15
    Woman
    Acceptance

Maxine Chernoff   17
    The Possible
    Cuchulain

Susan Cohen   19
    Golden Hills of California
    Quiver

Elizabeth J. Coleman   21
    Fearless

Gillian Conoley   22
    Election Year
    The House of Secrets

Lucille Lang Day   26
    Love's Seasons
    After Catastrophe
    Wanjina

Sharon Doubiago   32
    In the Lake
    Still in the Lake, Mama

Camille T. Dungy   35
    What I know I cannot say
    Characteristics of Life

Iris Jamahl Dunkle   39
    On Hearing that the Radiation from Fukushima
        Has Reached the West Coast
    Instead of the cross, the Albatross
        about my neck was hung
    Hole in the Sky

Sandy Eastoak   42
    River

Terry Ehret   43
    Enough Hardness
    Night Sky Journey
    Half a Woman

Annie Finch   46
    Amulet for Brave Women
    Pearl
    Being a Constellation
    In Cities, Be Alert

Molly Fisk   49
    The Life of a Grown-Up
    North of Tomales

Miriam Bird Greenberg   51
    Before the World Went to Hell
    Elegy
    The Arrival

Judy Halebsky   55
    Self Diagnosis
    Breath-hold Break Point
    Bristlecone Pine

Elizabeth C. Herron   60
       Holy Day 3

Brenda Hillman   61
       In a House Sub-Committee on Electronic Surveillance
       I Heard Flame-Folder Spring Bring Red
       Equinox Ritual With Ravens & Pines

Jane Hirshfield   65
       Let Them Not Say
       My Skeleton
       Engraving World-Tree with an Empty Beehive on One Branch

Jodi Hottel   69
       Unwritten Note

Susan Kelly-DeWitt   71
       The Moon Bee
       Callas
       The Crickets

Maya Khosla   74
       Migration Into Bhutan

Lynne Knight   75
       The Silence of Women
       Mothers and Daughters
       Willie Nelson's Braids

Danusha Lamèris   79
       Egg
       Insha'Allah
       Eve, After

Kathleen Lynch   83
       Canned Food Drive
       Letter to an Unmet Grandmother

Mary Mackey   86
       L. Tells All
       The Martyrdom of Carmen Miranda

Colleen McElroy   90
        Pumpkin Eaters
        The Alchemists

Jane Mead   93
        Money
        Untitled
        To the Wren, No Difference
                No Difference to the Jay

Toni Mirosevich   96
        Tool Time
        Back Up

Rusty Morrison   98
        our aptitude for perishing
        "our aptitude for perishing"

Gwynn O'Gara   100
        The Spirits That Lend Strength Are Invisible

Connie Post   102
        Taking you back to your group home
        Charlie, a Boy in My Son's Group Home

Kim Shuck   106
        Weight of Night
        Light in the Kitchen
        Going to Water in More than One Dialect

Hannah Stein   109
        They Can't, Can They,
        The Heat

Melissa Stein   111
        Racetrack
        Query

Jennifer K. Sweeney   114
        Snake in the Zendo
        In the House of Seals

Julia Vose   118
        Out of Center, Look Back In

Laura Walker   120
        genesis
        genesis
        genesis

Gillian Wegener   123
        Road Song, North on 99
        The Opposite of Clairvoyance

Arisa White   126
        Juvies
        Where Lakes Weren't Born

Toni Wilkes   128
        Resilience

Leonore Wilson   129
        The Tumor
        After a Line by Heaney

Kathleen Winter   131
        glamour
        Receptive Fields of Single Neurons in the Cat's Striate Cortex

Pui Ying Wong   136
        Seven Stars Path
        The Flag

BIOGRAPHIES AND ACKNOWLEDGEMENTS   139

Amulet for Brave Women

Women have voices it's time to believe in.
Wise women's strong words, spoken out clear and steady,
move us with generous ways of achieving.
Women have voices it's time to believe in,
braiding sweet worlds. This brave, loving weaving
is singing our lives back, and women are ready—
women have voices. It's time to believe in
wise women's strong words, spoken out clear and steady.

—Annie Finch

Introduction

In 2006, getting tired of driving to San Francisco or the East Bay every time I wanted to hear live poetry—which was often—I started the WordTemple Poetry Series in Sonoma County, California. My concern about no one showing up to hear poetry at that first reading was quickly abated when over 100 people crammed together to hear Jane Hirshfield, David St. John, and the "emerging" poet at the time, Jennifer K. Sweeney. A year later, I began hosting the monthly *WordTemple* on NPR affiliate KRCB FM. Now, in 2017, the series and the radio program are still going strong. For over a decade I've had the enormous pleasure of hosting a wide range of poetic voices. Well-established poets like Robert Hass, Dana Gioia, Nikki Giovanni, Carolyn Kizer, August Kleinzahler, Jane Hirshfield, Kay Ryan, Ishmael Reed, Michael McClure, Diane DiPrima, Alicia Ostriker, Al Young and many others have taken the stage alongside poets who were celebrating their first books or were with small independent publishers. After the first few months, a local, Sonoma County poet always opened each evening with his or her own work.

When the presidential election was in full swing in 2016, it was believed by many that this country would have its first woman president. This is when I got the idea to publish an anthology of women poets who either read at the WordTemple Poetry Series or were guests on my radio program. It was to be, in part, a celebration of this historic election. When the election took what we see now as an inevitable turn, I almost dropped the project. It seemed pointless, like so much did at the time. But I quickly changed my mind. Why on Earth should women have one less place to be heard now? The invitations to submit continued to go out and here we are.

There are women poets who have read at WordTemple that are not included in this anthology. This is not my choosing. The late poets Carolyn Kizer and Leslie Scalapino are just two poets I had a special fondness for whose work is missing from this book. Others either couldn't be contacted or couldn't respond to the invitation in time to be included. Fear not! This anthology is incredibly rich, diverse and filled with brilliant emotion and craft.

The title, *Know Me Here*, comes from a line from Devreaux Baker's beautiful poem "Invocation for Spring": "Know me here, where the wind dreams of us." From poems such as "Characteristics of Life," by the wonderful poet Camille T. Dungy where she writes "Ask me if I speak for the snail and I will tell you/I speak for the snail" to Arisa White's "Juvies" where "children are behind locked doors," to Mary Mackey's "The Martyrdom of Carmen Miranda" (*"chica chica boom chic"*), the poems in this anthology represent so much of our shared lives, interests and concerns, and they do so with full attention to what each poem needs to do its job: make the reader *feel*. Perhaps one of the more chilling poems at this time is "Unwritten Note" by Jodi Hottel in which a Japanese American relative learns "President Roosevelt has ordered our removal." This is not an anthology of political poetry, and yet it is. It can't help but be. The poems are by women, and they are appearing in the first year of a presidency that finds Margaret Atwood's *The Handmaids Tale*, Ta-Nehisi Coates' *Between the World and Me* and George Orwell's *1984* flying off the shelves for good reason.

It's difficult to express the amount of gratitude I feel for all the poets who have entered my life over the past dozen years. You have challenged me and enriched my life in countless, wonderful ways. I hope this book will serve as a small token of my appreciation. Deep thanks also go to South Carolina artist F. Berger-Doyle for this book's stunning cover image.

Know Me Here is a labor of love, as most books of poetry must be. And without my life partner of the past 22 years, CJ Rayhill, none of it would be possible. To her, the big-hearted love of my life, I owe everything.

Katherine Hastings
Santa Rosa, California

Know Me Here

INVOCATION FOR SPRING

This morning we searched for the one knot left to untie
We wanted to clear the way for sweet sap to rise
in the trunks of lost places, so talk is unnecessary
and we fall into the medicine our lives have been trying
to feed us
Know me here, where the wind dreams of us
as her lost tribe
where the universe weaves our bodies together
as one fabric
and we open ourselves to welcome the spring
to enter as one wound, to exit as one healing
Let the syllables of the earth inhabit my pores
as my skin stretches out to receive this passionate embrace
the universe offers
when she bends over us to gather in her skirts of loss,
kneels to wring out her 1,000 handkerchiefs of despair
this is the way sky has sex with earth and a blue child is born
who climbs a ladder of stars to light the heavens with fire
Take my breasts, my bones, the gentle ache of remembrance
spring offers, make them your home
This is where the shy vowels and sleeping consonants of our lives
join tongues to speak the language that lives
in all the rooms of the world
so when we come together we are stung by the simple pleasure
of the earth's release
this prick or sting that jumpstarts our hearts into sparks
like rain lifted and pulled
when the sky says *No, don't fall*
and her animal mind whispers, *Yes, release, let go.*

WE SHOW EACH OTHER OUR SCARS

We show each other our scars, *think* Krakow at dusk
winter in the yard, lights like globes of fire
trapped in distant buildings, heat bundled in hands

Think the train through Yugoslavia, how the guards
pulled you off at checkpoint, guns slung across their chests

We show each other our scars, *think* the world as lover or
first love, first sex, the heat, the mouth. Years later,
longing mistaken for thirst

We show each other our scars, the clock hands move forward
in increments, time branded on our features, our features
precise mirrors of our mothers or grandmothers;

mine in babushka, overalls, hoeing in the garden,
yours more distant, a dream in quilted coats moving through
your yard. We show each other our scars, *think* distant lands,
filled with the porcelain faces of rivers broken into pieces by fish
against our legs

We are wading across with canvas packs on our backs
We show each other our scars, the world may stop spinning
sometime in the future may speak to us in a language
we finally understand but by then it will be too late

Somewhere there are two women lifting their shirts saying
my scar is on my left breast just over my heart
small smudge, the surgeon left behind this one
shadow trace like eucalyptus leaves at dusk or

mine is on the right breast, hooked under and curving
like a pavilion rooftop, like a smiling moon
a gardenia leaf floating in the pond of my body
moonlight ripples my water

We are standing in the world knee deep, chest deep
treading this flow that sounds like twigs
breaking against our windows

Together the world is standing in us, asking if we are ready,
do we want more, what can we bear to carry
what can we leave behind

Dancing at the Round House

For the Kashia Pomo Round House
Stewarts Point Rancheria, California

I remember driving the coast road
dusk sliding in the car
women's voices, strands unbraiding
like hair flying in wind.

I remember the smell of summer
trapped in twilight, shy blue,
growing dark at the edges of sight.
I remember driving through dust
the language of dirt, the beginning and ending place
coming in the open windows

I remember the smell of wood smoke
cradling the dreams of trees
the old woman sitting at the door
asking me if I was on my moon,
the way her eyes held small lakes
shaking my head no, ducking inside.

I remember the smell of the earth floor
something cool and sweet, unknowable
drifting up, finding a place to sit
bodies beginning to move, drums
somewhere behind me, whistles in front.

I remember that old woman
dancing in front of me, pulling me up
onto the roundhouse floor, laughing and saying,

Come on, girl, get up,

  dance,   dance,

Get up and dance

ELLEN BASS

THE ORANGE-AND-WHITE HIGH-HEELED SHOES

Today I'm thinking about those shoes—white
with a tangerine stripe across the toe and forceful orange heels—

that fit both my mother and me. We used to shop like that—
trying them on side by side. That was when there still

was a man who would cradle your heel in his palm
and guide your foot. Sometimes he would think he made a sale,

only to have one of us turn to the other—
and he would have to kneel again, hoping to ease another naked sole

into the bed of suède or leather. I thought those shoes
were just the peak of chic. And—my God—

you bought me a pair of orange cotton gloves to complete the ensemble.
Why is there such keen pleasure in remembering?

You are dead ten years. And these showy slippers—
we wore them more than half a century ago. The first boy

had not yet misted my breasts with his breath
and you were strong as a muscled goddess, gliding nylons

over your calves, lifting your amplitude into a breastplate.
Who will remember these pumpkin-colored pumps

when I die, too? Who will remember how we slid into them
like girls diving into a cedar-tinged lake, like bees

entering the trumpet of a flower, like birds disappearing
into the green, green leaves of summer?

REINCARNATION

Who would believe in reincarnation
if she thought she would return as
an oyster? Eagles and wolves
are popular. Even domesticated cats
have their appeal. It's not terribly distressing
to imagine being Missy, nibbling
kibble and lounging on the windowsill.
But I doubt the toothsome oyster has ever
been the totem of any shaman
fanning the Motherpeace Tarot
or smudging with sage.
Yet perhaps we could do worse
than aspire to be a plump bivalve. Humbly,
the oyster persists in filtering
seawater and fashioning the daily
irritations into lustre.
Dash a dot of Tabasco, pair it
with a dry martini, not only
will this tender button inspire
an erotic fire in tuxedoed men
and women whose shoulders gleam
in candlelight, this hermit praying
in its rocky cave, this anchorite of iron,
calcium, and protein, is practically
a molluskan saint. Revered and sacrificed,
body and salty liquor of the soul,
the oyster is devoured, surrendering
all—again and again—for love.

TAKING OFF THE FRONT OF THE HOUSE

I'm at the kitchen table, drinking strong tea, eating eggs
with poppy-gold yolks from our chickens, Marilyn and Estelle.
There's a red car parked across the street and my neighbor's gorgeous irises,
their frilled tongues tasting the air.
"Monsanto is suing Vermont," I say, turning the pages of *The Times*.
I say it loud because Janet's in the living room
in the faded chair the cat has scratched into hay
eating yogurt and the strawberries she brought home from the field
where she labors to relieve the tender berry of its heavy chemical load.
"What?" she says. She isn't wearing her hearing aids
so I take a breath and project my voice. And as I enunciate the corporate evils,
suddenly the front of the house is sheared away.
We're on a stage, the audience seated on the asphalt of Younglove Avenue,
watching this quirky couple eat their breakfast and yell
back and forth from one room to another.
And throughout the day, as I throw a load of laundry
in the drier, answer the phone, as Janet lies on the couch
reading *Great Expectations* and we bicker
about the knocking in the pipes and whether we really need to call a plumber,
I admire how the actor who plays the character of me
and the actor who plays the character of her
perform our parts so perfectly
in this production that will last
just a little while before it closes for good.
And when night comes, we smoke a little weed—something called
                                    Thunder Fuck,
which must be someone's high opinion of himself,
but in truth is quite nice, though we only take a couple tokes
since Janet's on blood pressure medication and she can't
do the way she did at twenty when she slung a goatskin bag
over her shoulder and wandered around Senegal in flip-flops.

As I reach for her, she says, "Now the audience can sit on the back deck
by the barbeque and this play can be called
The Old Lesbians Go to Bed at the End of the Day.
I light the candle her mother gave me for my last birthday when she could
still put on her lipstick and Janet pushed her around the store
                                        in her wheelchair.
And the dog's still on his mat on the floor of the closet because he's afraid
of firecrackers and took up sleeping there last 4th of July on top of the shoes.
The set is authentic—a messy stack of books on my nightstand,
on her side, reading glasses and the hearing aids that sit there all day.
And as she turns toward me and I feel again
the marvelous architecture of her hips, the moon,
that expert in lighting, rises over the roofline,
flooding us in her old, flawless silvery wash.

ELIZABETH BRADFIELD

PURSUIT

—*for Arctic Explorer Donald B. MacMillan*
Provincetown, September

All summer, town kids pose at the edge
of the pier named after you

and leap. I've just flown home from Baffin,
Mac. A month of spotting polar bears,

lecturing on tundra as raw wind shrugged us off,
then winter chased us down the coast.

But it's still season here, and so I'm at the gangway
loading a boat to look for whales.

Boys dash between pickups. Girls strut
the edge, do the same. No one throws coins for them,

but I know you jumped for the bright glint
tourists threw, and (I'm sure) for the thrill

of being watched do it. These kids leap
to break the hot September days and because tonight

they might find themselves midair, recorded
by some out-of-towner's gadget and posted online

for view-count and comment, their currency. Would I
have strutted, have jumped at their age, yours then? I can't decide.

At high tide, their knees are eye level from my place
on the finger pier. One girl wears a silver bikini.

It shines like ice on the horizon. I can't help but stare.
Suddenly, I see it is desire

that links us, that galvanizes
the thin substance of our ambitions.

Dispatch from this Summer

Lymantria dispar dispar

Frayed, moth-eaten, vulnerable. Those Florida dancers
gunned down & my young self coming out dancing & pathetic
fallacy (*dispar dispar*) crawls all over June's fresh oaks,

gnawing them to a February canopy. The news, bad
oracle, gnaws fact & rumor. Above, unrelenting
mastication, defoliation. *Lymantria,* 'destroyer,' all else gone,

you hump up even the stiff needles of pines. What will happen
come winter, no sun stored? Should we spray? Should
we shun social media? Avoid large aggregations? How

hot the birds must be, unshaded in their nests. (Guilty
thrill of peering down on them, black-billed cuckoos calling.)
Other wings. The white towering stagecraft of angels

sentry at Orlando's mourning. We consider what it would take
to pick the trees clean. Could we? The bark the grass the ground
writhes. In a grove in China, a grim documentary:

honeybees gone, people pollinate fruit trees by hand. I twitch away
from one caterpillar dangling from its thread, hanging by
the silk that brought it here, to the New World, to Massachusetts

even, because some merchant in 1869—while Grant
took the presidency and Elizabeth Cady Stanton spoke
before Congress and the Golden Spike was hammered

into Utah and the South fumbled through what's called
Reconstruction—thought *crop, harvest, riches* & hoped
the long, expensive trek to mulberry unnecessary. We gnaw

through news feeds. We post & share, unsure
if we are offering or consuming. In the forest, a constant
heavy frass. On my side of the river, healthy trees. Oak leaves

thick and dark. In the dance clubs near me, there is
dancing. But introduction, dispersal. In the week
after Pulse, in Massachusetts, 450% more guns like that gun

were sold. If you can stand to walk a narrow path through the leafless
forest, you can arrive at a circle of water that will allow your body
to be beautifully held, whoever you are. It's true, you'll have to return

by the same path, go back through those apocalyptic trees. If
I had waited a month to begin this poem, I would have begun
with the re-leafing, fuzzed red growth in late July, moth-flutter

among the trunks not angelic but like paper corners that didn't
get burned in someone's attempted or accidental. Is it too late?
Now, plastered to bark, the russet humps of eggs that I scrape with a stick
—vengeful, hopeful, despairing—even as they are being laid.

—North Truro, 2016

REPAIR

Drake Passage, Southern Ocean

Bracelet I've worn since I took it from
you, now broken. Two places. (each of
us? our separate journeys to this iced
edge? these months apart?) No warn-
ing. Sudden snag pulling layer & layer
on.

> flaw in a dream of this place
> now I've come

If guys in the metal shop can make pro-
pellers from scrap, they can fix this.
Chief engineer returns it. Unfixed. *Too
pretty. Too nice. Afraid they'll damage.*

> thing of shine, thing of shimmer
> worn through our wearing

I want them to marr it. Want it worked
below decks within walls of metal, deck
of metal, overhead, hull, & all metal
making us possible across the Drake.
Marr story. Storymarr. Repaired as we
left. Pounded whole as we pounded
north. Home. Look. Fixed.

WOMAN

I am not an aesthetic object —
I don't really care what color
looks good on me.

For I am what colors
the Earth most
beautifully.

My skin blends
perfectly with the sands.
My eyes flow with the seas.

My smile blooms with the flowers.
My light shines inseparably
with the sun.

My darkness glows
with the moon and the stars.
And when your eyes have opened —

you will see.

ACCEPTANCE

I never felt part of this culture,
felt there was a place for a woman.
Maybe I could live with some native tribe,
travel on to India, maybe
stay in France, or retire to Ireland.
Maybe, after Hillary became president,
I could be an American.

But then, we are all just visitors
stopping over on a very long journey.
I came here for a purpose,
I met the Great One,
I have tried to do my dharma.
May all be fulfilled as it was meant to be
and is.

MAXINE CHERNOFF

THE POSSIBLE

"The stationary blasts of waterfalls." Wordsworth

The moss-covered birds I clean
in the stream look at me clearly.

A baby floats by: Moses? — I am
texting you when the dream concludes.

So much to tend, oneself included,
liminal clouds leaking cold rain.

Location as anchor and ivy-filled
absence: the spoken as dirt's surest refrain.

Awake to subtractions, seasons of smoke,
Aleppo's horizons drop from the sky.

Your private museum contains this world,
which doesn't make sense, unless in a photo,

but no—it is here, where silk worms
tend it: a milk-colored shroud cloaking its wounds.

Cuchulain

You wind up in limbo with liars and thieves who fear you, then
sew your own shroud. The exit a portal: you must grow wings.
And like crickets in season and crows at dawn, or the moss at your
feet feeding the stream, you are small and of things, as if heaven
or whatnot were the simple yard of a house in spring. Must you
believe? In sewing, in patience, as vines cover the windows and
you let them. Come in, you say, to the wind at the gate. You scatter
your weakness, splayed on white sheets, no homecomings, hearth,
or register. You mend what needs fixing, taking your cue from
autumn's trick of divesting, here and not here at once.

Susan Cohen

Golden Hills of California

This light began in lamentation,
but I don't want to think
about the unmaking, the burning
hopes and homes a hundred miles
from here. This light is strangely
sewn with honey as if thimbled
from the flight of bees. It drifts down
through maples and the cedar,
burnishes our scarred floorboards
to yellow oak this morning,
our walls to butter. In the fabled state
we live in, somewhere always is on fire—
dry grasses torching, shingles searing,
latches melting, miles of forest
reduced to the single syllable of ash—
while elsewhere that combustion blends
light and gold we can savor like wine,
which also begins with crushing.

Quiver

My body, ...
it is not the earth I will miss,
it is you I will miss. – Louise Glück

I say good riddance to my body,
its conspiracy of veins
and bowels and vertebrae.
I can trust a deer to pick its way
through trees, a daffodil
to bully its way through frost. Once,
I saw the silhouette of a baby seal
held inside the translucence of a wave,
like a portrait in a locket. How quartz
threads through rock, and a heron
threads through air then lands
and stills to a piece of quartz.
The way even weeds flower. Just now
the dullest brown bird appeared,
clumsy at our feeder, and picked
at soggy seed. I watched the quiver
of its tail while it fed its hunger.
Need I say bodies must be fed?
I say the earth is the body I will miss.
Even if I could only touch it dis-
embodied, send a shiver
down the outstretched limb
of a single eucalyptus.
Even if I could touch down only
in the linear brittle body
of a dragonfly, one evening,
some rank bog, skim
the skin and flit.

Elizabeth J. Coleman

Fearless

I want to be a surgeon, my son announced,
but *since I'm scared of blood,*

I'll be a blind surgeon. And I who am scared
to let myself paint, will be a blind painter.

And for fear of mucking up my words, I'll be
a poet without hands. For I am the daughter

of an engineer who was not allowed
to be an engineer, but I no longer know

what is fact and what is myth.
To honor my father, I will not die until

I've painted every New York street, written
an ode to each one, and taken the Circle Line

twenty times around our island, drunk
on cotton candy. The man on the phone

from the Philippines dealing
with my computer crash, keeps saying,

Now Elizabeth, I want you to remain calm.
Instead, I think of the acolyte Buddhist monks

sent nightly to the charnel house
to see what awaits us, and I am not afraid.

ELECTION YEAR

Four seasons one day, I was followed, viewed,

liked, leitmotif of a bra strap

warm as sun on my back, the gentler part
of maintaining my breasts' parallel

rhetoric, store windows shiny
a bituminous black surface under wet leaves

"eternity" (lower caps not
 mine) stenciled on boarded-up shack,

freakish actors on the snowy

television.

Last backup 12 days ago.

Since we can't sleep, we float
top the groundwater,

genital side up.
Seared, burned off, eyed,
red tape

makes good
bedpost bondage, or won't someone

blindfold me in the gauze of this forever so I can see
since I
count nothing

in all of the above
observed
under the rifle scope of a pedestrian—

I will use the darting ink

of a barn cat's sheen. The phone's
lorikeet

tone. When I
called out
to you,

you remained you, and we
walked the tangled cables,

karmic auras of undisclosed locations
within this entourage's

darkening seawater where the booths arrive,
                    and we're allowed to indicate

how when it comes to the unspeakable,
we're apprentices

in the afternoon.
Hamburgers
in an old auditorium.

Halibut,
lime,
fish taco.

Let's go home, cowboy.

Everything's good again, we have inventory,

we're going to

warm everyone
from the grave

even in some
nowhere town, ask

why were you here

what did you want

who are you beneath the cream
under your eyes
their hollowing circles

whirlpools of

who doesn't get the bends of when
"they" say "we"
"I" can taste "us"

in the razorblade in the apple, in the car wreck holding everything up
on the freeway, the everglades of

who better not.
Forget us not.

The House of Secrets

don't listen to her she is the dead "me."
in an inky negligee with black lace and no underwear, feeling a little
                                        invertebrate only,
with the same pint of ice cream devoured in the nineteen oughts.
we had spent only half a lifetime together but the quotient
                                        had forgotten the sum.
minutes quartered and hung in a buzzing, pointed treachery—then sleep.
come morning, a squirrel scampers off with a mouse by the neck.
the floor feels aquatic, absorbing heartbreak's sunken gut.
thin reeds at one's ankles barely skirt hallway's groove and path.
why speak?
all has to be said over and over until it turns into nonsense.
thin reeds at one's ankles barely skirt hallway's groove and path.
Narcissus to Echo, "is anyone there?"
Echo's only available reply, "is anyone there?"
Narcissus (tearing himself away), "Let's get together."
"Let's get together," Echo
echoes, empties about.

LUCILLE LANG DAY

LOVE'S SEASONS

After Sappho

Fragment 4

Four valves direct blood flow through the heart
in one direction so long as we are fully
alive. Can I ever let go? I think I can,
though for now, yellow star tulips for me
are worth it all: small suns to shine upon
the forest floor and light up your lovely face
in April. Come near, until we're touching.

Fragment 18

Everything turns to summer, enabling us
to speak in the colors of ripe peaches
my tongue caresses slowly while
storytelling in the orchard enchants us,
and a man laughs at something no
greater than a windfall in a storm.

Fragment 19

In October she waits for a vision
before she offers sacrifices to gods
not committed to having good intentions.

Stepping softly, she walks beside me,
hiding her face, for we know neither
our hearts nor the work of our souls

that might bud in the future, in any season
despite the lark's bid for glory in spring.
She loves me. Please say this is so.

Fragment 25

She left me when snow was falling,
and from now until spring I expect
no meadow rue, nothing so pretty.
I can't forget the color of violets,
fleeting yet returning each year.

Note: This poem incorporates the words of Sappho's
fragments as translated by Diane J. Rayor (*Sappho*,
Cambridge University Press, 2014).

After Catastrophe

Go to sleep. You need your dreams
as much as ever. Maybe more.
When you wake, make yourself a cup
of coffee, Conscientious Objector,
Certified Fair Trade and Organic,
a blend of Guatemalan, Ethiopian
and Sumatran beans. Do not
avoid the newspaper: no matter
how upsetting, you need to know
what's going on. Remember that
the redwood tree is still alive
even though it has fungal cankers
and you must keep pruning away
infected branches. So too with
society, which suffers from fear
and hatred, ancient diseases
that must continually be cut away.
Give the plants on your deck
some water. The geranium, fuchsia
and impatiens are still blooming
even though it's nearly winter.
Find solace in their resilience.
Then take your grandchildren
to a movie, *The Eagle Huntress*,
to remind them and yourself
that the Earth is gorgeous, even
when cold and dangerous, that
societies can evolve and change,
allowing a young girl in Mongolia
to take on a role once filled only

by men. Think about that girl
with an eagle perched on her arm
and ask yourself what you can do
to ensure that spring will come
again, with all the stars in place.

WANJINA

After paintings by Alec Mingelmanganu,
Harvard Art Museums

What are they doing here
at this museum at Harvard,
with their haloes surrounding
mouthless faces with owl eyes?
Wanjina belong in ancient rock
in northwestern Australia.

In southeast Turkey, a Kurdish
suicide bomber rams a truck
packed with explosives into
a checkpoint, killing eleven
people, wounding seventy-eight.

Did Wanjina emerge thousands
of years ago from the deepest
places of Ocean and the vastness
of Sky, on the other side of Earth,
to sit on these walls, watching over
strange people who stand silently
before them, as though in prayer?

Police officers stop a black man
whose car has a broken taillight.
When he reaches for his ID,
they shoot him and he dies.

According to the Mowanjum people,
the Wanjina are invincible.
These stippled beings will send
lightning, floods and storms to those
who break laws or disrespect them.

The father of a six-week-old girl
with a crushed skull and fractured
arms, legs and ribs is charged
with murder and felony assault.

The Wanjina have come far
to tell us past, present and future
are one, that time is an ocean
where we swim like so many
diatoms and protozoa, and riding
the ebb and flow of tides, we must
seek wisdom and compassion
as we drift and roll in the beauty
of this perilous cold sea.

Sharon Doubiago

In the Lake

Every night I'm in a hurry to lie down.
I just go down

Mostly red. Must be blood I'm floating around in, bumping into
body parts. My tendency to gore you so hated, but Mama
there's love here, too. I don't narrate. I'm
narrated. Swimming

around in the blood streaks
across your face like warpaint your last days.
I wouldn't call this the ocean. This is a lake. I wouldn't call this
dreaming. I'm learning to die, you still showing me how.
I go under free at last of your seven year old daughter's vow
to live one year older than Moses when he entered the Promised Land.

On my first birthday after you're dead I find you in the hospital.
Your old lung has to come out.
"It's very hard," you say in your meekest voice.
I hear a baby crying BYE-bye   BYE–bye

I turn on the light to write this. Your great grandson wakes, holds me
from leaving the bed. The smile
washes my face, seven years old, so seldom now
does he hold me.

You call out again, as you did that last afternoon
stranding me between the kitchen and living room
"I can't die yet!" I dive deeper

to know this boy who shines through like the sun
warming the surface. Today I will feel
with my grip around the weeds in your neglected yard
the anguished screaming of the roots, all
who've ever been here. My heart

is broken for life, Mama,
but you'll be relieved to know I'm happy in your lake.
When I pull the covers over
the same covers you covered me when that girl, I just
go down, float around. Drink wine and am narrated. This
is where I come from, not the ocean but Earth's heart. Friends

send me sudden post cards, "I keep dreaming you. Are you
okay?" Together we enter the lake.
This is not the ocean, but a man
running his fingers through my hair

And again that moment I'm brought back up
carrying your old lung

*

STILL IN THE LAKE, MAMA

I grieve you most in sleep when the sun
you so loved goes down. I go down
into the night, the shock
and the dark and the spirit and the questions, the
questing. Six months later you're still upstairs.
I sleep inside my dream, a baby
asleep. Then come up
through the long hours where I've been, what
has happened. Read awhile, not wanting
to go back in. But then

into pure dark, hear my voice saying so loud it wakes me,
"I love you, Mama."
This is not the sea, this is the big still deep lake, the black sky
I've never been in before, but knew
too well.

WHAT I KNOW I CANNOT SAY

We sailed to Angel Island, and for several hours
I did not think of you. When I couldn't stop myself, finally,
from thinking of you, it was not really you but the trees,
not really the trees but their strange pods, blooming
for a while longer, a bloom more like the fringed fan
at the tip of a peacock's tail than anything I'd call a flower,
and so I was thinking about flowers and what we value
in a flower more than I was thinking of the island or its trees,
and much more than I was thinking of you. Recursive language
ties us together, linguists say. I am heading down the road.
I am heading down this road despite the caution signs
and the narrow shoulders. I am heading down the curvy road
despite the caution signs and the narrow shoulders
because someone I fell in love with once lived somewhere near. Right there,
that is an example of recursive language. Every language,
nearly every language, in the world demands recursion.
Few things bring us together more than our need to spell out
our intentions, which helps explain the early-20th century
Chinese prisoners who scratched poems into walls on Angel Island,
and why a Polish detainee wrote his mother's name in 1922. I was here,
they wanted to tell us, and by here they meant the island
and they also meant the world. And by the island, they meant
the world they knew, and they also meant the world they left
and the world they wanted to believe could be theirs, the world they knew
required passwords. Think of the Angel Island Immigration Station
                                        as purgatory,
the guide explained. He told tales of paper fathers, picture brides,
the fabrications of familiarity so many lives depended on. Inquiries
demanded consistency despite the complications of interpretation.
In English one would ask: How many windows were in your house
in the village? How many ducks did you keep? What is the shape

of the birthmark on your father's left cheek? In Japanese, Cantonese,
Danish, Punjabi, the other answered. Then it all had to come back
to English. The ocean is wide and treacherous between one
home and the other. There can be no turning back, no correction
once what is said is said. Who can blame the Chinese detainees
who carved poems deep into the wood on Angel Island's walls.
Who can blame the Salvadoran who etched his village's name.
Few things tie us together more than our need to dig up the right words
to justify ourselves. Travelers and students, we sailed into the bay,
disembarked on Angel Island. I didn't think about you.
Which is to say, the blue gum eucalyptus is considered a threat,
though we brought it across oceans to help us. Desired first for its timber,
because it grows quickly and so was expected to provide a practical fortune,
and when it did not, enlisted as a windbreak, desired still
because it is fast growing and practical, the blue gum has colonized
the California coastal forests, squeezing out native plants, dominating
the landscape, and increasing the danger of fire. I should hate
the blue gum eucalyptus, but from the well of their longing,
by which I mean to say from their pods, you know what I mean
I hope, their original homes, from the well of their longing
blooms explode like fireworks. I love them for this. Do you hear me?
I absolve you. You are far too beautiful and singular to blame.

Characteristics of Life

A fifth of animals without backbones could be at risk
of extinction, say scientists.
        —BBC Nature News

Ask me if I speak for the snail and I will tell you
I speak for the snail.
              I speak of underneathedness
and the welcome of mosses,
                        of life that springs up,
little lives that pull back and wait for a moment.

I speak for the damselfly, water skeet, mollusk,
the caterpillar, the beetle, the spider, the ant.
                                I speak
from the time before spinelessness was frowned upon.

Ask me if I speak for the moon jelly. I will tell you
              one thing today and another tomorrow
        and I will be as consistent as anything alive
on this earth.

              I move as the currents move, with the breezes.
What part of your nature drives you? You, in your cubicle
ought to understand me. I filter and filter and filter all day.

Ask me if I speak for the nautilus and I will be silent
as the nautilus shell on a shelf. I can be beautiful
and useless if that's all you know to ask of me.

Ask me what I know of longing and I will speak of distances
        between meadows of night-blooming flowers.

                    I will speak
        the impossible hope of the firefly.

                        You with the candle
burning and only one chair at your table must understand
        such wordless desire.

                        To say it is mindless is missing the point.

On Hearing that the Radiation from Fukushima Has Reached the West Coast

Some days the light hits the green hills just right
and the cows stand guard against what's left of
sun: tangled in the syrupy, golden
light. Reminding me, I am passenger
on this trip of life. Blue bell sky. Rough hills
swelling toward sea. They say the air isn't
innocent anymore. It storms with what
we've done. Beauty has a way of making
you forget there was ever a threat. How
could this honeyed light contain a little
death? And even if, how could you look away?

Instead of the Cross, the Albatross
About my Neck was Hung

After Charmian Kittredge London aboard the Dirigo, 1912

Had we believed in omens, had we known
the way the albatross would stretch over
the cool deep that had seeped into the pools
that kept the thrashing reptiles of our minds sated.
On deck, the bird stood ten, perhaps twelve feet,
wings, a muscular arc. What filled my head
was my cavernous room still being built
at Wolf House in Glen Ellen—how the bird
could have soared between thick knuckled rafters.
How I wanted to kill it and did. How
I brought it back. Then, months later, when startled
awake by Eliza's screams, by the low
moan of loss from Jack, I looked out at
the ridge where our home had once stood, saw it
stoking like the heart of the mountain cracked
open—I remembered that bird, saw its ghost
fly out from the smoke.

HOLE IN THE SKY

After Charmian Kittredge London aboard the Dirigo, 1912

On nights when we search for mountains
of Magellanic clouds, the sailors punch holes in the sky.
Coal sacks. Darkness so deep and velvet it pours back
into the telescopic eye.
By day, I walk the deck on wet, bare feet.
Sharks circle our ship. Until one is hooked
and hoisted onto the deck. The men smell blood,
gather to rip its rough belly open. Pour what's left
of it – body and chum – back into the churning sea.
And somehow, it swims on, crooked, spelling
a dark sentence back into the deep.
What comes are the others. The like-bodied.
The like-minded. Until what was body,
what was sandpaper skinned and muscle taught blooms
back into a mountainous cloud. Into the deep.

Sandy Eastoak

River

in the dark forest rivers roar,
cutting canyons through the trees.
jagged conifer cliffs soar
& fall to soft willow knees.
obstacles of log & stone
slow the water's downward dash,
swirling pools where eggs are sown
& baby salmon glint & flash.

under the willows a curving shore
eats soft ripples from the breeze.
boatmen cunningly explore
quiet eddies at their ease.
a heron balances alone,
ignores a turtle's sudden splash.
she hunts beyond the shallow zone
where baby salmon glint & flash.

such loveliness grew long before
the centuries of human squeeze.
now we struggle to restore
pristine rivers such as these.
where the firs and willows have grown
lovely, thick, tangled & brash,
cool, clear waters purl and drone
so baby salmon glint & flash.

the willows playfully adore

the solemn beauty eagle sees.
where water sings a godly tone
the baby salmon glint & flash.

ENOUGH HARDNESS

Black Head, County Clare

1.

Along the scoured bluffs at Black Head, the sea
has left many shores. I cross each, lifted
slowly into the limestone sky. I have walked here

when the sky-doors flew open and poured
another sea down the glacial clints. But my feet
planted themselves like roots

of the blackthorn. And here I'll stay long seasons,
until the stone itself gives back
the rhythms of the churning tide, and I

climb down its many shores
like steps in time, toward the first water,
cradled in stone.

2.
My shallow roots have left me
far from the homeward path. There is more truth
marching in the dark wind, in the blessed wind.

A black chuff calls, "Be silent! Be still!"
And so I stop reaching for what costs me so much.
Parched by the salt of the sea inside, I begin to be a temple
(there is no birth as hard as this). Ah, will I come to be an orchid,
blooming among rocks? What can I teach myself,
but to be a meadow, bathed with stony kindness.

Night Sky Journey

For me the sky is no home, is a vast sea of sadness
where once my heart fought and died, and lies, not buried,
but rocking in a boat anchored between two mountains.
All night the moon's sharp edges slice the heart in my breast.
All night I break into pieces again and again, waiting for daylight
to gather me, waiting like one alone at a station,
waiting for the train of memory to rumble up into daylight,
into a morning threaded by trains, the bustle of each day's arrival.
I turn and turn in this night of errors, fractured
by the burning light of my heart, fractured by the wind
that blows here in the vast country of sleep.
No one knows what the wind illumines,
what shapes form in the little anxieties that each hour
follow behind us, ringing like bells.

HALF A WOMAN

> after *The King of Masks*, directed by Tian-Ming Wu

The young Sichuan opera singer sits in the tea room with the master mask-maker. "I am only half a man," the singer says, because he lives on stage as a woman, sings a woman's feelings, holds the attention of the military general who comes to each performance night after night. Half a man, half a woman. And therefore nothing but his quiet dignity and his giving heart.

A woman, too, might be half a man, might know everything a woman needs to know about her arms and what they want to hold. And yet, such a woman hides her heart, the small, pulsing sea-anemone of her heart beneath her multiplying arms that the sun turns brittle. Hides the halfness of herself she wakes up to out of her darkness where she is something whole, something floating and membranous in the deep, unlighted currents of her dreams, something that cannot carry its beauty to the surface whole.

Such a woman, half a man, must hide beneath the masks the master brings, poling up the wide river each morning in his flat boat of lacquered chests filled with the faces she waits to wear.

Annie Finch

Pearl

Reaching with eyes, they covered her as a girl,
leaving a grain of gaze, that irritant stare
women must cover everywhere, like a pearl.

Even alone in her own room, she curled
back from the windows gleaming with their glare.
Reaching with eyes, they covered her, as a girl,

and stopped her eyes as their long look unfurled
taking her in as if she belonged there,
a woman, covered everywhere, with pearls

draping her throat. And then she learned to whirl
before the mirror, pierce her ears, and twine her hair.
Reaching with eyes, they covered her, as a girl

covers herself and hunches to a coil
spiraling from the voyeur. But beware:
women cover everything, like pearls

orbed into life. A living ocean swirls;
we reach through it to spiral everywhere.
Reaching with eyes, they covered, in the girl,
what the woman covers: everything, like pearl.

Being a Constellation

Heavy with my milk, you move
your compact body, though I hold
you dense under a constellation
whose sparse lights ache over you.

If, looking up, you recognize
the shadowing of curves that cast
down towards my belly, and the way
my nipples travel, like two stars

twinned by your eyesight; if my arms
take night, and keep it from the sky,
if my night voice can stop your cry,
I'll be the Mother over you.

You are a question, small and dense,
and I am an answer, long diffuse
and dark — but I want to be sky
for you so, like the stars, I lie,

holding my far lights wide and flat
in pictures for your eyes to take,
spaced easily, so you can catch
the patterns in your sleepy net.

In Cities, Be Alert

You may hear that your heartbeat is uneven
and let new tension climb around your shoulders,
thinking you've found the trick for going mad.
But try to keep a grip on where you are.

Remember: all around you is pure city;
try to stay alert. On the wide streets,
so empty late at night, streaking in glass,
the color of an alley, or the fall

of a sideways flicker from a neon sign
may utterly and briefly disconcert you —
but as you go, you'll find that noise is worse.
Prepare for noise. But never scream. Even tensing

ears too far in advance can sharpen sirens,
and as for horns…When you're back to
your normal rhythm after such encounters,

just try to stay alert. You'll never know
exactly who is coming up behind you,
but the sudden movement of pedestrians

will finally, of course, be what disarms you.

THE LIFE OF A GROWN-UP

Because I have to look up the spelling of hors d'oeuvres every time.
Because now and then rain still comes in under the north-side window.
Which blisters the paint, and weeks later it pops and peels
And no one I've found so far understands how to fix it.
Because this isn't how I imagined the life of a grown-up.
Because cheese and crackers for dinner, fish soup for breakfast.
Because sometimes bed at 6:30, sometimes 2 in the morning.
Because no one else is there to figure it out.
(Or to argue, either, a blessing.)
Because patience, endurance, inventiveness, humor.
Because planting trees for your own shade is such an honor.
Because cat barf and young male renters who tighten the cap
On the laundry soap so you can't wrest it open.
But then also haul the rolled up rug out to your car and pay you
The rent on time, every time. Smiling.
Which is good because no one else is going to figure it out.
We all know the world is unlikely, and not to eat too much
Butter. Though some of us do. Because the world
Unlikely year after blossoming, burnishing year.
Because the way love smooths the edges, softens
The grief, teaches us lessons we hoped never to have to learn.
Because compassion is slow and a long time coming.

North of Tomales

Some places are built of wind. You hear of people going mad,
the ceaseless sound and motion scraping sanity away. Any softness
pared and honed, whatever's blown across the surfaces abrading
so that colors fade and shine is muted, smoothness pocked.
And if there's salt, as here, where an ocean meets the narrow bay,
sheep fences will green their lee sides with lichen, metal instantly corrode.
The rocks survive both wind and lashing wave, cypress bend
but stand. Even poppies sometimes grow in sidewalk cracks.
If you last, the constancy becomes a kind of music, a reminder
under sun or fog or in the winter rains that you exist. You are here
to be buffeted against. Like love. Half metaphor, half prayer.

MIRIAM BIRD GREENBERG

BEFORE THE WORLD WENT TO HELL

Before the world went to hell my sweetheart
worked at a diner
near the marshes and before that was a physicist in the desert, but now
we were on the move;
the whole country had uprooted—she recognized an old woman
soaking acorns in the river
as a colleague from her first laboratory job. Southerners
had migrated bodily north
leaving fabric shreds in the mesquite, and the west was on fire.
                                             My sweetheart
steamed a pot of wild mustard flowers
by the roadside, rain sizzling on the lid. Her shadow,
my breath, the afternoon
that moved on forever: people theorized the earth's orbit
was off kilter, time
had stopped moving right, and suddenly though we'd brushed snow
from our walkways
that morning, the sun began to rise two hours earlier. Smoke
gathered in corners
of the sky, and the peach trees budded, then blossomed
and bore fruit
in a week, but the fruit was mealy and filled with larvae. This was back
when we had walkways,
our own houses, cars, my sweetheart was a stranger
crisp in her lab coat
and I had never tracked a deer all day then field dressed it
and dragged it home
across wild grass grown tall over an emptied city.

ELEGY

Early on in the city
on weekends claimed by fog
I came back to your farmstead,
your emptied creek-side
shanty house,
from my laboratory wage work
with pockets full of micropipettes
and stolen white gloves as if to outfit a regiment
of ghost butlers
in an imagined antebellum manor
neither of us, if offered, would inhabit—
but I still saw the manor's cut crystal
glinting in night-frost on the fescue
beneath persimmon trees
where great horned owls left
bones to bleach. These nights
lately—with the fine rain singing
through ragweed, through mulberry
we'd kept for feeding ducks, the silkworm
farm we planned
to someday have—I swim
the wild wheat that shines
like a lake to far back acres. I unstring
my jewelry, tarnishing from its work week
even still—in the city of sooted brick and grimy
air—from my neck
and wrists, spread the legs
of the wooden-runged ladder and hang
it in arcs inside the fig bower's
ribcage or hay rick,

displayed like ceremonial
specimens pinned to felt-lined glass cases
by the fig's knobby twigs. Deprived of ceremony
I find nothing
in my hands but unmoored
symbols: one week I caught junebugs in a jar every night
to feed the ducks,
or once so methodically burnt old letters
from lovers and the First National Bank alike,
as if a prayer summoning spirits
to the occasion could ever come
from cynics' lips. We forget
the histories cat's-cradling
between us, unwillingly
as algae on river stones
loosed downstream rejoins indistinct matter.

THE ARRIVAL

We spoke the same language. No,
we did not speak the same language.
We believed in the same gods. No,
we didn't believe in the same gods.
The lavender fields where we first arrived
were forever symbolic to us; the scent
not somnolent but a promise
of our new future. No, none of that.
The boat we stepped ashore from,
it was burned behind us. Perhaps
they thought our people had only one
and if we couldn't leave, no more
would come. No, it was not our only boat,
but though we hoped others would follow,
none did. The reeds we used to make our first bed
bent easily, and we laid together
in it on a cliff side with paths traced
across the rock face. We snared birds
in nets and roasted them on a spit;
we ate greens picked from sparse rock
outcroppings. We kept a torch aflame
all night for protection. We slept safely.
No, our fishing line disappeared
from its reels, our earrings
from our ears. Finally the blankets
that covered us vanished and we woke
shivering in the inky night. The stars
turned slowly around us, night birds
swept their ugly shadows across
the stony path, and we waited.
No, we did not have to wait.

SELF DIAGNOSIS

They named her Cassandra, as one who can see the future

> *daughter of Priam, daughter of Hecuba*
> *daughter of Troy*

delusion: a conviction to something impossible

folie à deux: psychosis passed from one person to another

a miracle: worms eating compost, plum blossoms under new snow

> *daughter of a reed loom*
> *daughter of a cotton wood vine*

newspaper code, radio waves, the rush of air in a bus door opening

the Martha Mitchell effect: when real events are diagnosed as a delusion

> *Cassandra of Watergate, Cassandra of Troy*

one topic delusion: baseball, weddings, credit cards, fidelity

delusion: a kind of dream

> *daughter of dandelion and thistle, daughter of rubber trees*
> *daughter of dragonweed and murr*

BREATH-HOLD BREAK POINT

We sink, that's the thing
unless we've learned how to float

there's a page in the manual for how to rescue
two people, underwater, clinging to each other

Sister Carla calls the men at San Quentin *our brothers*

Phil lives by something called radical honesty

we lose track of which way to the surface

they say it's like being drunk
there's a euphoria, a kind of bliss

remember: air bubbles float upward

born in lupine, in Willamette Valley, in Oregon
this year's six Blue Fender butterflies

how many do we need
to count ourselves as having survived?

make these questions into a cloud
up in the canopy
this bark, a balm

under the low branches of pine
fluttering a bed of needles and resin

from here clouds form out of
vapor to water, a patch of cold air
they move across the sky
into warmer air, then disappear

BRISTLECONE PINE

— with two haiku from Basho

Mission Blue butterflies lay their eggs in lupine
monarchs in milkweed

they migrate 2,400 miles
from the high mountains of Mexico to here
they travel in months and years
they live for six weeks

Mom says, *one lifetime isn't enough*

feed me a broth of chanterelles
make me forget with snowmelt and fireweed

butterflies can barely see
so they flutter toward any movement

even a long day
is not enough singing—
for skylarks

remember: by the time they come back
it's five generations later

pupa, Latin for doll, between a caterpillar and a butterfly

remember: skylarks only sing while flying

remember: each tree has a name

bristlecone pine live for a thousand years
unless there is fire or disease or people near by

sugar pine is named
for the sweet gum
that collects on its trunk
as a way to heal a wound

a butterfly sanctuary isn't for butterflies
it's for milkweed and lupine

    over the field
    clinging to nothing
    a skylark sings

Elizabeth C. Herron

Holy Day 3
November 28, 2016

I found the long lost moon and stars
in the corner of my suitcase
strung on a gold chain
just in time for Christmas
I'd been thinking I was an upright isosceles
of bones exuding light
before I burst into flame
and my skeletal shape
a remnant of what I thought
I was
collapsed
into ash and the bits of bone so hard to burn
you find in the box they give you
after cremation
of your beloved dog and
this is the answer
it seemed to me at last: I am nothing
the empty hearth
the burned building birds fly through.

IN A HOUSE SUB-COMMITTEE ON ELECTRONIC SURVEILLANCE

It would be lovely to ask water to investigate
        domestic spying so i put myself in a trance
                right here in Congress holding a bottle of H2O
from California so when the Principal Deputy Assistant
        Attorney General reads *probable cause to believe*
                the water shakes its curly geyser brain &
when he says *need to close the gaps* it shakes times 3 until its letters
        break & splash to the floor of the Rayburn Building
        OHH-OHH-OHH-OHH-OHH
        OHH-OHH during the report about reading
        your email. Maybe it's not your email.
From the 2nd row it's possible to see white ridges in his
        thumbnails while he holds *surveillance has to be*
reasonable as the prong-prong molecules <<<< of water
        trickle through the carpet to find
        the vault where the Electronic $urveillance
Modernization Act, the Terrorist $urveillance Act, the National
$ecurity $urveillance Act & the Foreign
        Intelligence $urveillance Improvement &
        Enhancement Act are stashed to hide them
        from the mobs of 1772. There's a secret
in every act down there. i hear some water interview the ants
        who make the basic laws of the land & while
the Deputy reads *ferret out terrorists* the water interviews
        a ferret under Capitol Mall that can't quite
streamline operations in the ruddy soil. Perspective is gained;
        the trance method seems to be working well.
i can see half a heart in each Congressman;
        i can see the Deputy has a shaving cut &
a sunbeam shining through the skin of his left ear,
        it's feeling rather prone, the light, its pink
        the color of winter robins' legs that

makes me want not to hate him. It's the tendency
        of light to change itself. He probably has two
    kids & lives in Fairfax near where Whitman's
mockingbird spends winters; he was sprinkled with birth,
    his death floats near the secrets he can't read.
There's a clue in every word down there. When he says
        has to be reasonable the droplets
            splash their skinny necks & swelling Buddha
bellies & break to make CAPITOL HILL spell I TOLL
        or TOP AL ILL. You at home, what do you feel.
    You can vote by calling 1-900-it's-either-too-fucking-
        late-or-too-early. There's
a secret in every century that likes it
    if you shout. There is time for our little secret.
There is space for the secret spilling out.

I Heard Flame-Folder Spring Bring Red

       to the jack-knifed tulip—
smart shy underachieving red,
       its idle set too low…Week of quinces
leaning into plum. Teaching *The Aeneid*
for the twelfth time. Is Virgil anti-war? One
student notes "Virgil really cares"
    what the weapons are made of: Turnus
aims his spear of ilex & burning hemp —
    Geese sound like puppies overhead,
the leader barking in the skinny rain—

Ceaseless Empire Trojan Roman
Ottoman British U.S.A., treating tribal lands
like layers on a big old onion. Hard to be cheerful
    at work. Fuck cheerful. Women
in Kandahar make $2 a month; our people
tweet & sleep through the wars,
    our soggy purses lie open, the eyes
    of the dollar bills stare up from the floor—

Mother, send your owl to the West
    for the soul has hung
      the great hurt on a branch
& the omens will take it away.
      One of its wings hangs down
a little bit, its markings fitly imagined,
its feathers all prayed about—

Equinox Ritual With Ravens & Pines

—so we said to the somewhat: Be born—
   & the shadow kept arriving in segments,
  cold currents pushed minerals
up from the sea floor, up through
coral & labels of Diet Coke blame shame
     bottles down there—
  it is so much work to appear!

unreadable zeroes drop lamps
    as mustard fields [*Brassica rapa*]
 gold without hinges, a vital
     echo of caring…On the census,
just write: *it exists!* Blue Wednesday
     bells strike the air like forks
  on a thrift store plate,
& the shadow moves off to the side…

In the woods, loved ones tramp through
  the high grass; they wait in a circle
    for the fire to begin;
they throw paper dreams & sins upon
      the pyre & kiss, stoking the first
  hesitant flame after touching a match
to the bad news— branches are thrust back
across myths before the flame catches—;
ravens lurch through double-knuckled
    pines & the oaks & the otherwise;
a snake slithers over serpentine
then down to the first
    dark where every cry has size —

(*for EK & MS*)

JANE HIRSHFIELD

LET THEM NOT SAY

Let them not say: we did not see it.
We saw.

Let them not say: we did not hear it.
We heard.

Let them not say: they did not taste it.
We ate, we trembled.

Let them not say: it was not spoken, not written.
We spoke,
we witnessed with voices and hands.

Let them not say: they did nothing.
We did not-enough.

Let them say, as they must say something:

A kerosene beauty.
It burned.

Let them say we warmed ourselves by it,
read by its light, praised,
and it burned.

My Skeleton

My skeleton,
who once ached
with your own growing larger

are now,
each year
imperceptibly smaller,
lighter,
absorbed by your own
concentration.

When I danced,
you danced.
When you broke,
I.

And so it was lying down,
walking,
climbing the tiring stairs.
Your jaws. My bread.

Someday you,
what is left of you,
will be flensed of this marriage.

Angular wristbone's arthritis,
cracked harp of ribcage,
blunt of heel,
opened bowl of the skull,
twin platters of pelvis—
each of you will leave me behind,
at last serene.

What did I know of your days,
your nights,
I who held you all my life
inside my hands
and thought they were empty?

You who held me all your life
in your hands
as a new mother holds
her own unblanketed child,
not thinking at all.

Engraving:
World-Tree with an Empty Beehive on One Branch

A too beautiful view rejects the mind.
It is like a person with a garrulous mouth but no ears.

When Basho finished his months of walking,
he took off his used-up sandals,
let them fall.

One turned into the scent of withered chrysanthemum,
the other walked out of the story.

It's only after you notice an ache
                    that you know it must always have been there.
As an actor is there, before he steps in from the wing.

Another of Basho's haiku:
a long-weathered skull, through whose eyes grow tall, blowing grasses.

They look now into a photograph,
a scraped field in France, September 1916:
men bending, smoking, gleaning the harrowed rucksacks for letters.

War, walking, chrysanthemum, sandal, wheat field, bee smoke of
                                    camera lens, war.

They're in the past, yet we just keep traveling toward them, then away,
carrying with us the remnant, salvageable,

refugee honey.

JODI HOTTEL

UNWRITTEN NOTE

The news is on everyone's lips
like flies gathering on excrement:
President Roosevelt has ordered

our removal. Will we be
taken from our homes like vermin?
I know it must be a misunderstanding,

gossip spread in these
harsh times. I choke
on acrid laughter.

It is not possible.
After all, I served
my chosen country in the Army,

in the Great War. So I go to see
my longtime friend and sheriff
of Monterey County.

It is no joke, Hideo. You'll have to go.
He can't look me in the eyes.
When he finds my body hung

in this rented room, with
my certificate of honorary citizenship
expressing honor and respect

for your loyal and splendid
service to the country,
he will understand why

I could not allow
this noble country to tarnish
its honor, or mine.

SUSAN KELLY-DEWITT

THE MOON BEE

The moon bee is made
of frost. She wanders

the halls of underleaves
at midnight

and sucks the shine
from silvered pistils.

Her sting is quick,
a frozen

bite—iced
venom, if you cross her

path like chance.
Tonight

she hums
in a groove of shadow,

solo.
She breathes

the groves
of deep song in.

CALLAS

The calla's made for you to paint…
        —Anita Pollitzer to Georgia O'Keeffe

She's out in a dusty field
painting the white funnels
stubbed with nubs of butter

color, her ivory shirtsleeves
spattered in oils, scrolled
up over thick, useful wrists.

No matter if the field's in her
mind: There's a burning, a wind
wild as loneliness; an open space

between two faraway ridges.
The callas unfold slowly,
reluctantly. She grows stubbornly

toward each flower, like an eye
toward its only light.

THE CRICKETS

They kick up a fuss in our hearts
These hot delta nights

These delta nights
As the starlight pours down

In rivulets, in currents, in staggering streams
A silent salient chorus of dying light

These hot delta nights
The crickets belt out their sex song, their hope song

The forewings of love, now that's a concrete thought
These delta nights, these hot, delta nights

The life wish written in concrete
The life wish signed, dated, sealed, and delivered

Maya Khosla

Migration Into Bhutan

Himalayan winter. Aloft
above blue-shouldered grandmother hills
black-necked cranes are keeping an annual promise.
They circle the monastery three times
then land close to the deep wetness below it.

A pair of cranes swings forward
into a million-year-old pirouette, wings flaring.
They bow. Call. They pick at the meaty bog.

From every east window, the monks lean out
and answer their winged ancestors with prayers:

that the mountains will preserve their secrets
from wind, from descending ice-sheets,
that the cranes will counter their vulnerability
with hatchling sequels of themselves.

But the cranes are unable to sense a dwindling
in their number.
They can't see a steady fire cracking them open,
scattering their short days.

They simply hear in their own blood
a whistling, empty landscape
immense as the Tibetan plateaus they left behind.

LYNNE KNIGHT

THE SILENCE OF WOMEN

Finally the silence of women began to disappear.
It crumbled like old bread.
It evaporated like steam from broccoli.
It rose like the scent of turmeric from kitchens.
It mixed in with birdsong.
It flew over rivers and oceans.
It settled in prairies, it poured out
like water trapped in leaves.

The silence was one language.
All the women on earth spoke it:
they had mastered the tongue.

But it vanished in the sound of vacuum cleaners.
It lifted like smoke from chimneys.
In winter, it covered the snow. It was white, then,
so at first no one noticed. *More snow*, they thought,
longing for spring. When spring came,
the silence burst into cherry blossoms, plum blossoms, apple.
This world of ours! the women cried.

And their stories rushed out like breath
held almost too long—

MOTHERS AND DAUGHTERS

A mother should be able to sum things up.
It's the adult way, the helpful strategy.
I myself have always been a loss at this.

The sky, I told my child, the sky is there
like a thought you never finish. My child
looked skeptical. After several more instances

of this, involving the sea, menstruation, love,
my child took to reading late in bed, under
the covers with a flashlight, though I made

or would have made no objection to her light
staying on. This is not, of course, how she
remembers it. She remembers prohibitions,

categorical imperatives, inflexibility
worthy of the spines of her best books.
I was blind to most of this: a side-effect

of my failure to sum things up. I saw her
discontent but believed I could do nothing
to ease it: children were by nature discontent

or what would move them to discover the world
for themselves? Now that my child is grown,
I spend my days summing up. Useless activity.

I name my follies, my inadequacies. No mother
is without them. But if I mention this to my child,
my grown child, she thinks I'm making excuses

for not having provided her essential elements. *Look at the sky*, I tell her silently. *Keep looking. There. You will never get to the end of this.*

WILLIE NELSON'S BRAIDS

Max wasn't dreaming of another
kingdom, or worrying about the afterlife.
He wasn't even hungering for bones.
He was just sleeping his old dog sleep.
Sometimes his whines seemed almost human,
little come cries in the silence of the afternoon
while I lay reading on the bed above him.

A month, two at the most, the vet said.
A good life, as dogs' lives go, even if
he had been neutered early. But he'd lived
with million-dollar views and great composers,
though the only music he liked was Willie Nelson,
whose crooning usually made him hump my boot.
Now not even Willie got to him. He just lay

like more of the rug, frayed and dying.
My mother was dying, too, and I knew that
sometimes when I spoke of Max, I meant
my mother. That old try-to-fool-your-psyche
transfer, like reading stacked *New Yorkers*
to take me back to all the years I'd read them
during visits to my mother in St. Augustine.

Before her fall. Before I began to pray for
another kingdom where I'll find her,
where things will go on as they were,
the dog chasing after a bone, my mother strong,

Willie Nelson's braids dark brown again,
straight down his back like roads
we can all keep travelling forever.

EGG

And here it goes, again, the body
hauling one out of the ovary
like coal from a mine,
lifting it up from the mother lode
by the frayed wires of late progesterone.
I can feel the familiar cramp
of effort it takes to summon
a lone ovum: my forty-odd year friend,
my little homunculus, my dwindling sack
of genetic gold. How many moons
have I carried you deep inside the secret stores?
You came into this world with me,
down the narrow birth canal, buried in the girl
until the first blood. And here we are, still
performing our same old reproductive ritual,
more formality than use. A mock battle
staged by aging warriors, turned allies.
Childless, I've called myself—
a son in the grave, and another seedling
gone to ash. But now I see
how far we've traveled together,
me and my specks of yolk,
sealed in the same skin,
spores caught in their pinules
beneath the fern's curled fronds,
barnacles on the back of a whale,
nuggets of ore covered in silt.

INSHA'ALLAH

I don't know when it slipped into my speech
that soft word meaning, "if God wills it."
Insha'Allah I will see you next summer,
the baby will come in spring, insha'Allah
insha'allah this year we will have enough rain.

So many plans I've laid have unraveled
easily as braids beneath my mother's quick fingers.

Every language must have a word for this. A word
our grandmothers uttered under their breath
as they pinned the whites, soaked in lemon,
hung them to dry in the sun, or peeled potatoes,
dropping the discarded skins into a bowl.

Our sons will return next month, insha'Allah.
Insha'Allah this war will end, soon. Insha'Allah
the rice will be enough to last through winter.

How lightly we learn to hold hope,
as if it were an animal that could turn around
and bite your hand. And still we carry it
the way a mother would, carefully,
from one day to the next.

EVE, AFTER

Did she know
there was more to life
than lions licking the furred
ears of lambs,
fruit trees dropping
their fat bounty,
the years droning on
without argument?

Too much quiet
is never a good sign.
Isn't there always
something itching
beneath the surface?

But what could she say?
The larder was full
and they were beautiful,
their bodies new
as the day they were made.

Each morning the same
flowers broke through
the rich soil, the birds sang,
again, in perfect pitch.

It was only at night,
when they lay together in the dark
that it was almost palpable—
the vague sadness, unnamed.

Foolishness, betrayal,
—call it what you will. What a relief
to feel the weight
fall into her palm. And after,
not to pretend anymore
that the terrible calm
was Paradise.

KATHLEEN LYNCH

CANNED FOOD DRIVE

We lived in the lucky world —
not the far place where flies
sipped at eye corners
of children too weak to cry.

A camera showed that world to us
on posters. But we were children.
We wanted most to not be those
others, with their terrible bones.

We spoke of them wide-eyed, with
what we thought was tenderness.
But our words came in a different
register, as if to speak of such

betrayal by the grown world
could bring a harm of great immensity
upon us too. We got to choose
from the cupboard. We gave

what we hated — beets, peas,
mushrooms. Our dreams
were not of rice. The moon
laid light on our bicycles propped

against the porch. Sycamores
became our giants standing guard;
the overgrown shrub, our fort.
We thought we understood

what was required. Even crouched
beneath our desks during air raid drill,
we said one prayer for the fear,
one for recess.

McClellan Air Force Base sent forth
big-bellied planes that rattled our windows.
Evenings, we took to the streets shrieking
with joy, rode madly fast around the block.

We collapsed on the lawn breathless, the earth
cool beneath us & pounding hard,
as if it had one great heart.
As if it was ours.

Letter to An Unmet Grandmother

They said there was nothing of yours left
but I found a black & white under the lining
of a rat-gnawed jewelry box. Until now you existed
only in stories, the hardest one the slow-leaked
secret about your suicide. First, I thought you look
too strong for someone who would do that, but
I know deep things are never that simple, and guess
it's more about luck, or something nameless.

Now I'm a grandmother myself—Maga to our flourishing
boys. I've seen seven decades of family history unreel
with its tangles and splices. But as a child I believed
that if only you'd known me, if you'd waited for me
to come along, I'd have been able to charm or cheer you
out of it. I'd pretend we'd come to visit, and you'd rush us
with your wide embrace, and somehow I'd be the one
who would end up on your lap, and you'd untwine my
waist-long braids, brush and brush until my hair
rose up electric to meet your hand.

That dream's behind me now, but the afterlife of its wish
burrowed in as if it had come true. I will say this: I love
knowing that once you carried my mother in your body,
and she was born with half of me in her, and that means
in a way I lived in you once, like a picture waiting in an
undeveloped roll. And the dog in the photo — your dog
I suppose. How gently you lean to the mutt, offer a treat
from your apron. I can almost see you ruffle her fur
in the next frame; almost hear you coo, Good girl, good girl.

Mary Mackey

L. Tells All

I wanted a man
but they were in
short supply
so when this big white
swan followed me home
and announced
"I Am Zeus, Lord of All Creation,"
I crooked my finger at him
and said
"come here, Bird Boy,
let's give it a try."

at first
I have to admit
it was fun
his soft breast
the excited squawk
the way he beat his wings
frantically
like an umpire gone bad
but basically
it was an act of
desperation

we had nothing in common
his feathers made me sneeze
I was afraid to fly
he was married
(of course
they all are)
and we even had religious differences

what can I say?

and then there were his other
women
Io, Europa, Semele
(not to mention the
sluttish little pens he picked up
in the park)

we started to have
terrible fights
I called him an overstuffed
pillow and threw seed
in his face
he threatened to migrate
the usual stuff

by spring
we'd both had enough

one night
while we were sitting
in a Greek restaurant
I told the old cob I'd always
be his friend
but I just couldn't handle
interspecies love

(I lied, of course
the truth was
I'd already started to see
a duck
on the side)

The Martyrdom of Carmen Miranda

If you want to look like the quintessential hoochie coochie
girl, thereis no better costume to have than the Ultimate
Collection Carmen Miranda Outfit
        —Ruthie's Costume Company, Advertisement

in that foreign land
you were always a joke
the fruit basket hats
the crippling high heels
the bare midriff
the broken English
the carnival mask smile
done up in pompoms like a pet poodle
wearing your past on the inside
like a hair shirt
the Brazilian Bombshell
who could only say *hot dog*
moneey moneey moneey
does you like me?

never mentioning
the long hours you worked in the hat shop
to buy medicine for your tubercular sister
the bad marriage to the man who beat you
the miscarriages, depression, pills
the pain you felt when at last you came home
and discovered your own people despised you
for selling out to Uncle Sam

when your gay composer protested
your betrayal of Brazil by swallowing rat poison
you danced on like a frantic puppet
singing of the Afro-Brazilian gods
in a language no one understood

Chica Chica Boom Chic
Chica Chica Boom Chic

Carmen   like you we are all travelers
who set out believing we can bring back
something to make it worth the trip
money, love, hammocks, fame
something that will make us happy and whole
something that will heal our wounds
and give us peace

Colleen McElroy

Pumpkin Eaters

1.

these wives exude patience

their patience is misleading

an undertow threatens the current

each phrase coded with so much

left in declension an unhealed wound

a sotto voce complaint perfectly modulated

they speak without final punctuation

sentence endings indefinite without a break

the manicured table set precisely at seven

each dish to make him proud

their panther stripe folded on a closet shelf

in a house at the edge of everywhere

2.

in that house by the lake she is Mary

Shelley to his Frankenstein

she the subject being viewed upon the surface

upon which he the artist is drawing

evenings she decorates

the patio with dark silhouettes

a pose she holds sober or not

waiting for sunsets bloody tinge

she is the nation he the country within

aloud they read the classics

full of words only she can hear

dreams suspended in corpuscular light

.

THE ALCHEMISTS

in the former home
for wayward girls
the ladies today have gathered
to find their cores
they circle and circle coaxing
the spine
they try to remember all primal
moves and the alchemy of how
torsos flex and the knowing
of how joints bend
like waves against the shore
they master the movements
the dolphin the swan
and in the corners plants
quiver with attention
while ladies push muscles
past each creaking
past each reluctant arc
and plants of seldom bloom
pollinate in luscious
greening
leaves absorbing all loose
endorphs
and sweetened breaths
one drawn from another
plants and ladies
reaching toward light
both dancing on air

MONEY

Someone had the idea of getting more water
released beneath the Don Pedro Dam
into the once-green Tuolumne, —

so the minnows could have some wiggle room,
so the salmon could lunge far enough up
to spawn, so that there would be more salmon

in the more water below the dam.
But it wasn't possible – by then the water
didn't belong to the salmon anymore, by then

the water didn't even belong to the river.
The water didn't belong to the water.

Untitled

As is the name of the earth, goes this good one.
As is the name of the molten river.
As is the name, that river going forth.

The moon in the trees was a good moon,
The world in the sound-bite, a good world.
As in tunneling, the years went forth.

Narrow misses. Some bright star for stopping.

Madeleine gave me pomegranate seeds.
Betsey gave me strong tea with sugar.
Already we have suffered over the dropped fruit enough.

Already we have drunk the wine and suffered.

I have not yet come to a place of stopping.
You have not yet come to a place of stopping.
This is the way. Some people have hands.

Being a woman, you flow and keep.
There's a birthing-tent waiting on the plains.
This is the way. Some people have hands.

To the Wren, No Difference
No Difference to the Jay

I came a long
way to believe
in the blue jay

and I did not cheat
anyone. I
came a long way —

through complexities
of bird-sound and calendar
to believe in nothing

before I believed
in the jay.

TOOL TIME

(Organic machinery)

To get from here to there we need sharp tools – hacksaws,
lawn mowers – that will slice through red tape, duct tape,
the 18 minutes Rosemary Woods nipped out of Nixon's yarn.
To deal with the new skein of fools we want machetes to slice
away the folderol, the excess, like a deli blade slices the ham-
fisted *prosciutto*, paper thin, so we can see through the subterfuge.
Let's trim away the official detritus, delete it, our wheat bread
from their chaff. Everybody needs a tool. Even Mae West,
when meeting Dr. Death, said "Hey mister, is that a scythe
in your pocket or are you just happy to see me?" She cut
to the chase, made haste, then made love, not war, she didn't
suffocate fools gladly. To get from there to here let's buy
a new shredder or at least paper scissors to trim the dough
around the tin then slice ourselves a bigger piece of pie.

Back Up

Retrace your steps

If we could just back up a little, throw it in reverse, choose
not to round that last corner. If we could spring forward
and fall back, turn back the clock like a person turns a key

to relock Pandora's box, rethink the military advance
as one might turn back an unwanted pass, no whoopee
on the first date. If we could first tread softly then retread,

all the while carrying a small sized stick (we aren't naïve)
or walk backwards in snow, the footwork already laid out,
then I could step back from my defended position and you

from yours, we could unpuff our chests, remove our bullet-
proof vests, find proof there's still hope for a solution. To be
on the safe side we'll back up our disks, our opinions, our

plans, and then plan an alternate route, prevent a tail spin.
Don't get your back up, my mother always says, *or the fur
will fly*, and this is a no fly zone. What if, when someone

spit in your eye you turned the other eyelid and said *Back
at you*, without malice? If Sisyphus could *just do it* in reverse,
walk down the hill, the stone at his back, or if we could read

backwards and this time learn from history, maybe we could
turn the pages back far enough, before the world changed us.

Rusty Morrison

OUR APTITUDE FOR PERISHING

today a waxy streetlight   is timing out just when you
need it most & sunrise seems   meager godless as you read
about computer programs   that distinguish if prose is

written by men or women   based on the frequency of
words like *a the with & not*   though deeper analysis
to consider what this means   or its usefulness is not

assessed due to this study's   parameters which glow in
the highlight of your yellow   marker that soon dries all to
a dull sameness Jasper Johns   once made two observations

that you can't seem to forget
beware the body & the
mind

"OUR APTITUDE FOR PERISHING"

your every temporary   compromise will be inscribed
on a future that's been made   indecipherable by
the manipulations you   use to reposition its

likeness in the photos you   store but only to show more
new friends you probably would   not recognize on the street
here's mold that no cleaning will   remove a housefly shrugs sound

around this lonely room full
of what your objects won't tell
you

Syllable-counting constraint:

In the "our aptitude for perishing" poems (the phrase is a quote from
Maurice Blanchot), I'm working in a form that I created (seven-sylla-
ble segments; no punctuation; tercets until the last line; with its last
segment a single syllable).

I want to write about limits. But I don't want to just write *about limita-
tions*, I want to live inside limitation in the work and then see how I
handle it. I want event, not aftermath. Ann Lauterbach points out that
the "convergence of subject matter with form releases content." I've
found that this form creates a contentiousness in my use of syntax that
forces me to diverge from my more expected trajectories of thought,
and so it exposes a content with more contextual resources than I'd
had access to.

Gwynn O'Gara

The Spirits That Lend Strength Are Invisible

Navajo saying

The grandmothers came to me on the wind
the furious wind from the west they came
from the sun as I rocked and rocked
beneath the sky the sky of one color
pale as my baby's skin and as bright

I saw them and heard them as I rocked
and rocked for dear life coming out of me
coming down slowly out of me as I rocked
back and forth back and forth as he pushed
out of and back into me out of and back into me

The grandmothers came to me and whispered
Breathe Rock Wait Open
they came with the wind out of the sun
they came from their cave hidden in time
from their procession down to the sea
where they prepared me years before in dreams

They came and brought strength and peace so I
could rock into the dusk and on into the darkness
rocking and breathing and fighting the peaceful way
to let my baby deliver himself to me from his cave
their cave that is endless and built of moons

I rocked and I rocked and the grandmothers
came to me and whispered their words of power
to help me through the long disengagement of my son
on wheelchairs cornstalks mops and meteorites
they traveled and turned through the white sky
They gathered around my head in whorls of cooling
fire and they gave me water from the sun that
burned me cool and they took from me my
separateness no longer—not ever—would I be
sola and they eased me open to let out my son

So I rocked forward to become a mother
and backward to join them the ancient ones
holders of life bringers of life

Connie Post

Taking you back to your group home

It's the same ride
fourteen years have passed beneath the wheels

one hundred eighty-three miles
round trip

I think only the road understands
remembers the fierce quiet
on the way back

I used to bring the green blanket
but now you like the red one better
the halfway mark is the truck stop
where the hay field ends

when you rock back and forth
the car moves and at times, you laugh
even then, people stare
even from lanes away
they don't understand that a car
carries a trunk of untold stories

they don't understand how many times
I've made this trip
pulled away from the curb
groped for my sanity beneath the seats

I have raged at the fields that have no way of
making it better
I have counted the road signs
when an hour was a place to drown

each town I pass remembers
the way you looked at me out the window
the last Sunday good bye
the way my chest caves as the water
rushes in

there is this one town, though, that has walnut orchards
where the rows make sense
It flooded last fall
It's a place where you grabbed my arm once, suddenly
deep in the teeth of winter
I looked back and saw you,
wrinkling your brow, leaning towards me

eventually, all the cars around us disappeared
the road fell beneath the silence
and the orchards looking on
telling us to hold on
to inhale this hourless road
and to just keep going

CHARLIE, A BOY IN MY SON'S GROUP HOME

One Sunday a month
I would make the same trip
the ending always filled with good byes
– layered regret

each time before I left for the long trip home
I walked across the room
to find you
in your same chair
staring into space
as if the blank air knew some way to
apologize for the life you had

your eyes fixed, far away

I approached
held my hand flat open
and you would take hold of it

your young, textured skin spoke to me
in its silence
told me you knew
your family hadn't visited you
in six years

how empty the cove
of a palm, can seem

I often ponder those moments now

six months have passed
since we moved our son closer to home

but I can't stop thinking of you
still looking far away
hands folded
as the afternoon
falls on itself
trying to find forgiveness
for having left the morning
too soon

Kim Shuck

Weight of Night

Bare toes on battered
Hardwood on cracked
Linoleum the
Trappings the
Pretense that we don't
Actually exist in dynamic
Balance with this culture of
Manic autobiography the
Personal is public the personal is
Public half sleeping
Fingertips on kettle on
Hot tea mug all manner of
Closets become
Chat rooms support groups
Self-analysis become self
Harm we could pretend
Equity could imagine that in
Some time before now they
Couldn't disappear us can
Talk story can Ignore the press the
Undeniable force of
Hot water on skin the smell of
Shampoo of chill air the
Press of this
Not yet morning with the
Light shift coming the weight of
Night giving over in a few weeks it
Will come it will
Come

LIGHT IN THE KITCHEN

December arrives toiling and in this
Chilly wind scattered just
Hint of a morning I want people
Around me who have their own things to do and
People gone recently or years ago people who
Cannot be here in my kitchen for early oats and
Apple slices with spice and the view out my
Kitchen window of fantasy lights the
City from the hill without close up of what the
Wind blows into the new of this
Often difficult month I want to start this
Well I want to feed people something
Here in the warm kitchen where we
Don't have to talk if we don't want to

Going to Water
In More than One Dialect

This grandmother fire speaks in
Copal smoke in
Water vapor the fog
Sees me here and along the
Canal a handful of fire for
Company down the
Mare street stairs and I'm a
Hinge a complex connection between this
Curling breath of sage and this city of
Brick and water and grey grey
Stone this city of collecting I
Sing smoke and memory with a
Borrowed voice from the flames an
Inheritance a
Prayer

HANNAH STEIN

THEY CAN'T, CAN THEY,

they won't simply whisk me back to the star I
came from? Where I spent so many
millennia, unawake?

Now it comes time to stop orbiting, time
to draw a tangent. Straight line.
No more lies, even

to myself, no more picking at mystery like a tight
dress seam, needling the smallest
stitches, a slit where skin

shows through. More fruit, better air, a purer
tone. They will have to open to me like
the storm yesterday, when

I went out to the sky, caught violet, indigo,
gold. The end? The beginning?
Like a pheasant

up from a brushy fencerow, splitting light
with his wing tips, just before
he flashes from sight.

THE HEAT

Here is what you and I believed: black dome
of the nibbled sky, light flicking through,
and up there, following us as we drove—
                    a lemon slice

on whose barren scatter voyagers left plastic
bags of feces before lofting away in slow
parabolas. Which fiction feels most like truth:
                    the night

we made snow cheese? Or smashed the radio
with a hammer while its bizarre accusations
carried on insanely from your silver fillings.
                    I'm not yet

worn smooth from that undoing.
If I wanted to invent a small hole in
the universe and pull you through with me
                    at least

there'd be memory. I dreamt of my
grandmother last night, I was fixing up her bed,
brushing away crumbs, pulling the sheet tight.
                    My grandmother
could never take the heat, she would sit
fanning herself, blotting her neck with
a handkerchief. She liked you. She said
                    Marry him.

RACETRACK

Velvet and shit: I summoned it
and come it did. The horses' flanks
are rank with sweat and flies and I
remember you between my legs
achieving for an hour or so.
We parted on the best of terms:
the sweet unsayable loss that's gain
in drag. The day hurt a little
brighter for all that sharpening.
I have a turnstile heart; it opens
madly and shuts just so.
In morning cold, the horses'
breath takes on the shape of terrible
blooms. The hoof-stamps sound less
urgently. I'm not talking about my heart.

QUARRY

A girl is swimming naked
in dark water. She doesn't see herself
as graceful but the water tells otherwise,
the way it loosens and strikes
and burnishes. Exposed
ledges, rock's crumble on surfaces
and the surface of the water broken
by her body, marine and white.
There is also a freckled boy
contained in his body's wish
to outstrip but for now
mere stripling, too slight
for the shoulders and limbs
that pummel and thrash
to make himself bigger.
The girl and boy
pinwheel in the water
and do not touch
but are connected
by invisible currents
their bodies manufacture.
Her eyes are closed
but she knows where he is,
diving from the turtle rock
a little clumsily, the muscles
like lozenges
in his thin legs twitching
as they push off.
Days of this. Weeks.

Then, detaching itself from
sun, water, blasted rock
another body comes,
a grown man, all smiles
and cigarettes
and offering. I still dream
that the red-haired boy held my head
under water
to spare me what the man did.

JENNIFER K. SWEENEY

SNAKE IN THE ZENDO

Folded as letters about failure
from the future, we are too serious
in our attempt, wall-facing,
arranging small pillows with mudra hands.
Grace is not practicing being graceful;
it's emerging from the scrim of every discomfort
with greater discomfort.
Once I wept in my car and a woman knocked on my window,
then held me in the gray parking lot morning.
It was not extraordinary but when I grip the steering wheel
in terror, I see her hands reaching toward the glass.
Make everything part of the practice, the zenji says,
jay that swipes your toast,
cleaning toilets in the guest house,
forest fire sweeping down the valley
the monks rush to meet, unraveling their black robes
of fire hose. Until the sobbing starts.
A woman in the corner whose body
shudders whole each grief shock and wave.
Collective we, great erasure,
do we imagine we are shouldering her grief
in a silent and beautiful gesture or are we trying
so hard to do something right we have surrendered
compassion in the stone of the Buddha?
The zenji's reed snaps its mindful warning
against the wood floor as she sobs
the meditation pre-dawn into day,
our eyes coolly down.
And the morning after she left, a snake
slid its copper into the zendo,
between us, wall-facing, so dutiful.

Some kept sitting though most shrieked, ran out.
Oh we passed our judgment around
the breakfast table after with our talk
of koans. I let the jay take the toast
from my mouth like spitting out sacrament.
The snake could have been a metaphor
but it was also a snake.
Blood in the lotus, we were trying so hard
in our unhappiness and the mountains
were beautiful crumbling under an opera
of fire. If there was anything to hear,
keep afraid what is fearful,
hold what demands to be held.

In the House of Seals

Ano Nuevo Lighthouse Ruins

Abandoned on its eroded jetty,
the Victorian is gutted by windbreak,
waves and the pale ash
of salt and plaster.
A clean wind howls up the spiral
stair, rattling the vacant dumbwaiter,
the picture window, walls
bleached in sheets of raw sun.
What keeper's lantern once swung
the veranda to meet the shore-
tossed plot, what wrack
and beckon of Pacific tide
is now pilgrimage for elephant seals.
Given a home, they return
to the mecca of their kind
paddle into the blown out façade
to birth and die
in heaps of tender slack, skin
like buckled wallpaper.
Dear sitting rooms of milk and bone:
life keens starkly forward
while the dying nurse the dead.
Who knows what will become of us
receding behind white curtains
and what bright ruins might lean
from the pitch of night to shelter us?

To be so wanted

in the work of decay.
If given a home, I'll take this home.
If given a soul, I'll shepherd it
on the backs of seals
held in the bellows
of a graysound love.

Julia Vose

Out of Center, Look Back In

"Backed up roses bleed out the ends of my hair"
—Anne Carson, Decreation

In the living room's unlit afternoon
Dark within
She collapsed with groceries around her chair
Looked into the shadows
Scenes of old pain reeling on
Unaware
Seven pink rosebuds on tall stems
Water up to their shoulders in the glass
Breathed unseen
Until a late Autumn sunbeam glanced the eves
Ancient sun shot in
A lily pad of light
Floats those bound pink petals
In slow release
As if the heads of bathing girls in pink caps
Gesture together in a water ballet
Lit the roses themselves from within themselves
The source of pink light
An illumination
Happened upon
Whilst the Siamese dozed
Upon her faux leopard skin
All in a moment she remembers
She bought those over-large pink roses
To burst this temporary gloom
That pink of Grandmother's
Certainty

"This too shall pass, honey"
These very roses
No gift of apology or condolence
No celebration of anniversary or achievement
All
For the boon
Beauty is
Scaffolding invisible
Lit from within

LAURA WALKER

GENESIS

in the morning i shadow you with envelopes, and falling down
stairs our breath; the night as it moves. and the lines recede, a
thunder; and they are ecstatic in the aisles; and the boats are
righted and culled from the bearing deck

and the rain
and the dark paper map
and the lineage of small white instruments, arrayed by the door

and there were the ones who grew; and there were the ones
spacious in trees; and there were those who pressed into surface,
who suffered and were not to blame; who recorded the sounds of
slippers on floors, a traveling back to weather and rind

GENESIS

in the night i take your trees for my own. and we call to the
sheen, ourselves; and the nightbirds are light and pin-pricked.

and there was harm; and there was sun; and there was called
twice and a borrowing thick

and the lamplight
and the flare
and the ones who spoke tied up in trees

and the child who drew his name; and the child who wrote it; and
the pressing forward of animal shapes, a kind of dancing. and the
ones who suffered who were not to blame; and the waiting ones,
and the leaning ones; and there is every unfairness. and we who
cannot say it slowly, the fishergirl in murky waters, the branches
hovering there, a bird with a collared neck. and your hand against
the nursery door

GENESIS

in the beginning the sound of holes, and the weight of treason and
light paper streamers. and a hundredfold, and below; and the girls
with thickening braids, brought round at last to see the slick animal
caught in the rain. and the deluge; and the dark; and the story past
the window

and the window
and the stutter

and the thought was insubstantial, and stained; and the hands were
limpid, and fraught; and the children scattered in front of the wagon
like increasing wind. and the pen that drew your name, and the one
that didn't; and a child with a small box of crayons, not yet opened;
and the positioning of fingers and wrists

and my hand was a token of yours
and the trees, pulled backwards

GILLIAN WEGENER

ROAD SONG, NORTH ON 99

we are hushed
        and sequenced
we're the road
        we're the fence
mountains in the distance
        cuddled up
each peak has a name
        we don't know
as we don't know the names
        of the husk-dry grasses
we are hushed
        we are sequenced
first this town, then the next
        long blank betweens
what's not predictable
        is which store is shuttered
or which graffiti
        has faded to shadow
we are hushed by the heat
        sequenced by the map
led and humbled
        by the cracked and patched
by the pavement
        cracked and patched
we're hushed,
        we're slung-low
fence posts slap by
        count and lose count
swerve once for the prairie dog
        twice for the bees
we're hushed and sequenced
        we're low-slung and low

there's cloud glower
     maybe lightning, not rain
dust spins itself a frenzy
     a tipping tower
the radio gets only fuzz
     since the antennae broke
we're hushed, we're silent
     the road a throat song
          thrumming beneath us

THE OPPOSITE OF CLAIRVOYANCE

You feel like a fool,
not being able to spot the bird,
the little bird making all the noise
contained in the center of you.

When did the tree become such a maze?
When did leaves become this impenetrable?

It isn't what you thought, standing here
under the tired green and hoping
so hard it's like a knife inside you
peeling off the soft tissue of your lungs.

Look hard enough, you are supposed to see.
Think hard enough, you are supposed to understand.

No one talks about the cold pain when this doesn't happen.

A nail in the foot, and then
the tetanus shot to save you from the nail.

The little bird keeps shrieking — sounds broken —
and your hope is that winter will make plain the bird,

will knock the leaves from that tree with a fist
hard and merciless as God's
and make plain that crying bird.

ARISA WHITE

JUVIES

The children are behind locked doors. Metal
closed on no new air. And there is a window
that frames them. The jail looks better than
their schools. The order, they don't get at home.
They're raised on what-I-want-to-do. Look how
she dismisses, waves away the thought that her
mother gives a damn. Who they're calling dad-
dy is pimp is the same tired-ass conceit. She is
out there, each day, making her world. On-the-
block, around-the-way encounters are the halle-
lujahs to attest that "she's not enough." Regard-
less what her mouth entices, still can't shake
that two-thirds stuff, the ain't I woman, too.
And eventually there is a pop. There is death.
However, we name the transition from then to
now and again, there is shedding old to make
something known. That these children are not
far from their first breath.

Where Lakes Weren't Born

You eat crow, pomegranates—all those delicacies that open the palate to wounding. You have these lessons learned and you wonder when you can stop learning, stop being charged, pushed to your edge—you do not fear any edge. How rocky or serrated, rusted or cursed, you and the mirror need a break. No longer convinced that opposite attraction builds character, it creates lakes where lakes weren't born, pulls back the grass and leaves bald knolls. You're a pastiche of crazy-looking and are the least persuaded by the new art of you—your freak is off. The lights have gone unpaid, the woman who masquerades as a fish shows her tail, wants you to play her scales, but you are lit by worry.

Toni Wilkes

Resilience

Gray mist licks wax myrtles. A barking seal
echoes through the gardens. Somewhere
a canine answers. Then all is still.

I pass by a scratch, a flick of evasive
rustling. Chickadees stutter into flight.
At the world's edge, I am learning

to embrace possible, to move again
toward *encompassing, inclusion.*
Sea palms, their toes embedded

on isles of rocks — a world entire bend
to the ocean's veracity, stand to its ebb
as if engaged in a discourse on wholeness

knowing the flood of folding water
that bends, almost breaks them,
comes without intent or malice —

its streams pour nourishment into every
crevice.   We are all broken,
the bluff, myself, that man grasping his

walker, the woman beside him with vibrant
orange lipstick exclaiming "that man's
a bastard." At the world's edge

I am learning to see more openly.
And if I see us as broken, it frees us
both, to rise again in the lingering tides,

to welcome all that washes
over us and through us.

LEONORE WILSON

THE TUMOR

When the tumor in the brain
nearly took my child, I was not
a neat mother, I was fierce,
fierce and protective; I did not
want anyone to set foot in that room
with the infinite machines, the tubes;
I wanted his boy body
all to myself like the day
he was born, I would not
break down in front of him, no
I cradled his skull in my hands
as if it was the universe and it was—
soul, spirit and flesh, found honey
of my life, my life's goal;
and I told those messengers, nurses, angels
to protect him from the fire
as he was operated on;
my strong one, Samson,
as they cut his hair and made
a C around his ear— C for his alma mater,
for cunning, for courage, coming
round which he did, my son
gold and silver, gentle
tongue from which even now
I drink.

After a Line by Heaney

...a shiver of beaded gossamers when you took the children
out to play in the morning dew, and the light motes
streamed in the haw of the pasture, and the oaks
surrounded you strong as iron bedsteads, for you wanted
your brood to know the soil, to be like running harts,
their bare feet rising soft and slippery over the earth's cocked
face as the bats flew like flags from the roof's scaffolding
and the quail scattered into the blackberries overgrowth;
o tethered mother, if you teach them enough in your restlessness
for as their father built the house, you imagined the chop
of his trowel echoing down the canyon, you who fled
from the one room trailer in to the winter air smelling the scent
of lilac faint as a fox's breath while your brood stepped
in puddles of muck, picked toadstools, their young thoughts
frozen as sap, how you wanted to go with him but you stayed
kenneled and faithful in the mizzling rain, your back to cattle
as the small yolk of December's lambency broke new upon the meadows.

KATHLEEN WINTER

GLAMOUR

for Sylvia Plath

toofastblackcar
        too fast

to be replaced by one so much
more beautiful   of course it killed her

       (what you get, for trying to be a cupcake)

let sparrows harry the raptor
let murderess dip her blade

of grass in perfume

       every twisting strand of hair

    a rope could save
       or hang you

we have some things to work on mentally

of course : a phrase we usually won't need

clearly *generally* : iceberg lettuce of the language

Broadway star hawked coffee
in recovery

      of course in general coffee makes you

pretty   meet me at the Church of the Immaculate

Virgin

        corner of Beaver and Cherry

          toofastblackcar!

Flagstaff I told you so   if you're rich

you don't have to be friendly

        is anything better now?

at the time she died even the literati
thought arugula was a weed

RECEPTIVE FIELDS OF SINGLE NEURONS
IN THE CAT'S STRIATE CORTEX

start from being driven:
cats on their pedestals of fur and bone

     to striate structures of the cage

Livery say plates of limousines
delivering industrialists
     to fundraisers   across a bridge

I could have gone to Detroit
but I struck out on my own
to buy a hundred thousand dollar horse

     write-off of three legs
      & half the torso

take apart a human
     you have teeth   & glasses

     a skull cap   plastic bag of calcium
sand

over those empty shoes see a ghost
     of the body

     my father
rode a bicycle before his face was permanently
gone   saved in this idea
       I call my heart

* * * *

science thought it
legitimate in 1959
to flash a cat's eye
fierce with points
of light as needles
tracked the V1 region of its brain

first stage
of the visual cortex

              we want to know
              precisely how to see

among a trash of animals
        discovery was accident

one cat's brain excited
by straight lines
        by angles

* * * *

what does he care
        the candidate

        a wishful type of general

for events of war
        at the levels of cells and limbs?

your panting will kill you
if they hear it

from a forest at the edge
of town you listen
as soldiers finish

your friends with knives
                with points of light

                companions
        we have to get past being Man—

there are people so powerful
they go into war zones

and carry only cameras

PUI YING WONG

THE FLAG

On the roof of the old barracks
a row of air vents burr,
breathless as nuns praying.
A string of bird calls —
light starts trickling,
sleepers fret behind the gauze.

A string of katydid songs
stark in the foothills
of Tennessee,
maybe it was Morgantown.
There, the library in July was cool
like a nave. Tell no one. Desire
is the flag I open and fold.
My room alights in doubt.

SEVEN STARS PATH

In perfect alignment
there's peace

plough blade is for scything
off shadows

by elbows, shoulders, hips,
a new set of legs,

open a ball of map.

If the year turns to smoke,
assemble a feast
over the ruins.

Dreams are like fate,
you will never finish
fighting the thing

until armistice
wears time like a mask.

Biographies and Acknowledgements

Devreaux Baker is winner of the 2014 Barbara Mandigo Kelly Peace Poetry Prize from the Nuclear Age Peace Foundation for her poem "In the Year of the Drone." Her books include *Light at the Edge*; *Beyond the Circumstance of Sight*; *Red Willow People*; and *Out of the Bones of Earth*. She is a recipient of a Hawaii Council on Humanities International Poetry Prize, the Women's Global Leadership Initiative Poetry Award, and a PEN Oakland Poetry Award. She has been awarded several fellowships.

Ellen Bass's most recent book is *Like a Beggar* and her poems appear frequently in *The New Yorker* and *American Poetry Review*. A Chancellor of the Academy of American Poets, she teaches in Pacific University's MFA program. "The Orange-and-White High-Heeled Shoes" and "Reincarnation" first appeared in *The New Yorker*; "Taking Off the Front of the House" was published in *American Poetry Review*.

F. Berger-Doyle (cover art) is a signature member of the National Collage Society where she has exhibited and won awards. Flo has also shown and sold collage art and paintings around the U.S. She lives in South Carolina where she belongs to many groups, gives lessons in collage, watercolor and acrylic paint, and does commission work. For more information, see "Flo Doyle Art" on Facebook.

Elizabeth Bradfield is the author of the poetry collections *Once Removed, Approaching Ice* and *Interpretive Work*. She lives on Cape Cod, works as a naturalist, and teaches creative writing at Brandeis University. www.ebradfield.com. "Pursuit" appeared in Academy of American Poets Poem-a-Day; "Dispatch from this Summer" in *About Place Journal*.

Janine Canan is a poet, psychiatrist, volunteer for Embracing the World, and the author of 21 books including poetry, stories, essays, anthologies and translations. *Love Is My Religion*, a collection of spiritual teachings by Mata Amritanandmayi, will be published soon. JanineCanan.com and Facebook.

Maxine Chernoff is a winner of a 2013 NEA in Poetry and the 2009 PEN Translation Award. Her next book will appear with Omnidawn in 2018. Her collection *Here* was a Northern California Book Award finalist. Professor of Creative Writing at San Francisco State University, she chaired the department for 20 years. "The Possible" and "Cuchulain" appeared in *Fuzz* #3.

Susan Cohen's second full-length collection, *A Different Wakeful Animal*, won the Meadowhawk Prize from Red Dragonfly Press and was a finalist for the Philip Levine, May Swenson, Blue Lynx, Richard Snyder, and other prizes. She lives in Berkeley, CA "Golden Hills of California" and "Quiver" appear in *A Different Wakeful Animal*.

Elizabeth J. Coleman is the author of *The Fifteh Generation* (Spuyten Duyvil Press, 2016) and *Proof* (Spuyten Duyvil Press, 2014), finalist for the University of Wisconsin Press' Brittingham and Pollak prizes, as well as two chapbooks. She is translator into French of poet Lee Slonimsky's *Pythagoras in Love/Pythagore, Amoureux* (bilingual edition), Folded Word Press, 2015. www.elizabethjcoleman.com

Gillian Conoley is the Shelley Memorial Award winner from the Poetry Society of America for 2017. Her seventh collection, PEACE, with Omnidawn, was named one of the Academy of American Poets Standout Books, and was a finalist for The Los Angeles Times Book Award and the Northern California Independent Bookstores Award. Her translations of Henri Michaux, THOUSAND TIMES BROKEN: THREE BOOKS BY HENRI MICHAUX, with City Lights, was included in Publisher's Weekly's top 10 poetry books in Fall 2014. She is also the author of THE PLOT GENIE, PROFANE HALO, LOVERS IN THE USED WORLD, and TALL STRANGER, a finalist for the National Book Critics Circle Award. Editor and founder of *Volt* magazine, she is Professor of English and Poet-in-Residence at Sonoma State University.

Lucille Lang Day, publisher of Scarlet Tanager Books, is an award-winning author of ten poetry collections and chapbooks, two children's books and a memoir. http://lucillelangday.com

Sharon Doubiago's books include *Love on the Streets* (University of Pittsburgh). The two poems in this anthology are from her new collection, *Naked to Earth* Wild Ocean Press, Spring 2017). She lives in Mendocino and San Francisco.

Camille T. Dungy is the author of four collections of poetry, most recently *Trophic Cascade*, and a collection of personal essays called *Guidebook to Relative Strangers*. She edited *Black Nature: Four Centuries of African American Nature Poetry*, and co-edited the *From the Fishouse* poetry anthology. "What I know I cannot say," and "Characteristics of Life" both appear in *Trophic Cascade* (Wesleyan UP, 2017).

Iris Jamahl Dunkle is the current Poet Laureate of Sonoma County, CA. Her latest book is *Interrupted Geographies* (Trio House Press, 2017). Her previous collections are *There's a Ghost in this Machine of Air* and *Gold Passage*, winner of the 2012 Trio Award. Dunkle teaches at Napa Valley College and is on the staff of the Napa Valley Writer's Conference. "Hole in the Sky" first appeared in *five80split* literary journal.

Sandy Eastoak is a painter and poet intent on nudging herself and our culture back to harmony with all our relations. www.sandyeastoak.com

Terry Ehret is the author of four collections of poetry, most recently *Night Sky Journey*. She is one of the founders of Sixteen Rivers Press, and from 2004 — 2006 served as poet laureate of Sonoma County where she teaches writing. "Night Sky Journey" was originally published in *Night Sky Journey*, Kelly's Cove Press, 2011).

Annie Finch's eighteen books of poetry and poetics include *Eve*; *Calendars*; *Among the Goddesses*; and *Spells: New and Selected Poems*. Annie has taught and lectured at numerous universities and now teaches poetry-writing independently and in the low-residency MFA Program at St. Francis College in Brooklyn. "Amulet for Brave Women" was first published in *Cutthroat: A Journal of the Arts*l. All others in this anthology were first published in *Eve* (Story Line Press, 1997), Reprinted Carnegie Mellon Contemporary Classics Poetry Series, 2010.

Molly Fisk is the inaugural Poet Laureate of Nevada County, CA and the author of *The More Difficult Beauty* and *Listening to Winter*, as well as three books of radio commentary. She is the recipient of grants from the National Endowment for the Arts, the California Arts Countil, and the Corporation for Public Broadcasting. www.mollyfisk.com

Miriam Bird Greenberg is the author of *In the Volcano's Mouth* (Pittsburg 2016), winner of the 2015 Agnes Lynch Starrett prize for poetry. The recipient of fellowships from the NEA, the Poetry Foundation, and the Provincetown Fine Arts Work Center, she is currently at work on a series of poetic ethnographies of economic migrants and asylum seekers living in Hong Kong's Chungking Mansions. "Before the World Went to Hell" appeared in *Nashville Review*; "Elegy appeared online at Verse Daily; "The Arrival" was first published online at *Killing the Buddha*.

Judy Halebsky is the author of two collections of poetry, *Tree Line* and *Sky = Empty* which won the New Issues Prize. Originally fro Nova Scotia, she lives in Oakland and teaches at Dominican University of California. "Breath-hold Break Point" and "Bristlecone Pine" first appeared in the journal "Soundings East."

Katherine Hastings is the author of three collections of poetry, most recently *Shakespeare & Stein Walk Into a Bar* (Spuyten Duyvil, NYC 2016). She is the editor of *Digging Our Poetic Roots — Poems from Sonoma County* and *What Redwoods Know — Poems from California State Parks*, published as a benefit for the California State Parks Foundation. Poet laureate emerita of Sonoma County, CA, she founded the on-going WordTemple Poetry Series in 2006 and has hosted *WordTemple* on NPR- affiliate KRCB FM since 2007.

Elizabeth C. Herron is the author of four chapbooks, a book of short fiction, and poems currently in over a dozen literary magazines. She is a long-standing member of PEN and a Fellow with the International League of Conservation Writers.

Jane Hirshfield is the author of eight collections of poetry, most recently *The Beauty* (Knopf, 2015), long-listed for the National Book Award. She is a current Chancellor of the Academy of American Poets. "Let Them Not Say" first appeared in Poets.org *Poem a Day* (January 20, 2017); "My Skeleton" in *The Beauty*; and "Engraving: World-Tree with an Empty Beehive on One Branch" appeared in *The New York Times Magazine*, "A Poem and a Picture" Series," June 12, 2016.

Brenda Hillman has published nine collections of poetry with Wesleyan University Press, most recently *Seasonal Works with Letters on Fire* (2013), which received the Griffin International Prize for Poetry. She has co-edited many volumes and recently collaborated with Garrett Caples and Paul Ebenkamp to edit Richard O Moore's *Particulars of Place*. Hillman serves as the Fillippi Professor of Poetry at St. Mary's College of California. "In a House Sub-Committee on Electronic Surveillance" appears in *Practical Water*, Wesleyan University Press (2009); "I Heard Flame0Folder Spring Bring Red" and "Equinox Ritual With Ravens & Pines" appear in *Seasonal Works With Letters on Fire* (Wesleylan University Press, 2013).

Jodi Hottel's chapbook, *Heart Mountain*, was winner of the 2012 Blue Light Press Poetry Prize. A second chapbook, *Voyeur*, is forthcoming in 2017 from WordTech Press. "Unwritten Note" appears in *Heart Mountain*.

Susan Kelly-DeWitt is the author of *Spider Season* (Cold River Press, 2016); *The Fortunate Islands* (Marick Press, 2008); and seven small press collections. Her work has appeared in many anthologies and journals. www.susankelly-dewitt.com. "Crickets" was published in the online journal *Levure Litteraire*, Number 8.

Maya Khosla has written for the page, the screen, for performance, and for artistic works. Her publications include *Web of Water: Life in Redwood Creek* (nonfiction; Golden Gate Parks Conservancy Press); *Heart of the Tearing* (poems: Red Dust Press); and *Keel Bone* (poems: Dorothy Brunsman Poetry Prize, Bear Star Press). "Migration Into Bhutan" appears in her collection *Keel Bone*.

Lynne Knight is the author of five full-length poetry collections and four chapbooks. Her awards and honors include a PSA award, the 2009 RATTLE Poetry Prize, and an NEA grant. "The Silence of Women" appeared in *The Persistence of Longing* (Terrapin Books, 2016).

Danusha Laméris is the author of *The Moons of August*, chosen by Naomi Shihab Nye as the winner of the Autumn House Press Poetry Prize. Her work has been published, or is forthcoming in *The Best American Poetry; The American Poetry Review* and *The New York Times*, as well as other journals and anthologies. "Egg" appeared in *The American Poetry Review*; "Insha'Allah" and "Eve, After" appear in *The Moons of August*.

Kathleen Lynch is the author of *Hinge*, as well as the chapbooks *No Spring Chicken; Kathleen Lynch — Greatest Hits; Alternations of Rising*; and *How to Build an Owl*. She publishes fiction and essays as well. www.kathleenlynch.com. "Canned Food Drive" reprinted with permission of Poetry Magazine. "Letter to an unmet Grandmother" appeared in Poetry East.

Mary Mackey is the author of seven collections of poetry, including *Sugar Zone*, winner of the 2012 PEN Oakland Josephine Miles Award for Literary Excellence. She has also written fourteen novels, one of which made *The New York Times* Bestseller List. www.marymackey.com. "L. Tells All" appeared in *Breaking the Fever*, Marsh Hawk Press, 2006; "The Martyrdom of Carmen Miranda" is from *Traveler's With No Ticket Home*, Marsh Hawk Press, 2014.

Colleen McElroy's collections of poetry include *Winters without Snow* (1979); *Queen of the Ebony Isles* (1984), winner of the American Book Award from the Before Columbus Foundation; *What Madness Brought Me Here: New and Selected Poems, 1968–1988* (1990); *Travelling Music* (1998); and *Sleeping with the Moon* (2007), winner of the 2008 PEN Oakland National Literary Award. Her awards include grants from the National Endowment for the Arts, a Rockefeller Fellowship, and a Fulbright Creative Writing Fellowship.

Jane Mead is the author of five collections of poetry, and the recipient of grants and awards from the Guggenheim, Whiting and Lannan Foundations. For many years Poet-in-Residence at Wake Forest University, she manages her family's ranch in northern California. "Untitled," appeared in Banango Street (magazine) "Money" appeared in the book MONEY MONEY MONEY/WATER WATER WATER, Alice James, 2014 and "To the Wren," appeared in the book THE USABLE FIELD, Alice James 2008

Toni Mirosevich is the author of six books of poetry and prose, including, *The Takeaway Bin* (Spuyten Duyvil, NY). She is a professor of creative writing at San Francisco State University. Both of her poems in this anthology appeared in her collection *The Takeaway Bin* (Spuyten Duyil, 2010).

Rusty Morrison is the author of five books, including *After Urgency* (Tupelo), winner of The Dorset Prize, & *the true keeps calm biding its story* (Ahsahta), winner of the Sawtooth Prize, the Academy of American Poet's James Laughlin Award, the Northern California Book Award, and the DiCastagnola Award from Poetry Society of America. She has been co-publisher of Omnidawn (www.omnidawn.com) since 2001. www.rustymorrison.com

Gwynn O'Gara taught with California Poets in the Schools for twenty-five years, and served as Sonoma County Poet Laureate from 2010 through 2011. Her books include *Snake Woman Poems,* and the chapbooks *Fixer-Upper, Winter at Green Haven,* and *Sea Cradles.* "The Spirits That Lend Strength Are Invisible" appeared in *The Evansville Review, Volume X!X, 2009,* and *CALYX, Volume 25, no. 3, Winter 2010.*

Connie Post is the author of *Floodwater* (Glass Lyre Press), winner of the Lyrebird Award. She is a winner of the Crab Creek Poetry Award. Her poems have appeared in *Calyx; Spoon River Poetry Review* and other journals. "Taking you back to your group home" first appeared in *Calyx;* "Charlie, a Boy in My Son's Group Home" appeared in her chapbook, *And When the Sun Drops* (Finishing Line Press).

Kim Shuck is a protein. The latest of her four books is *Cloud Running In* (Taurean Horn Press).

Hannah Stein is the author of *Earthlight (La Questa Press)*. Her poems appear in journals ranging from the American Poetry Journal to Zeek. She lives in Davis, CA with her husband, the mathematician, Sherman Stein.

Melissa Stein is the author of the poetry collection *Rough Honey*, winner of the APR/Honickman First Book Prize. Her second book will be published by Copper Canyon Press in 2018.

Jennifer K. Sweeney is the author of *Little Spells* (New Issues Press), *How to Live on Bread and Music* (James Laughlin Award winner), and *Salt Memory*. After living in San Francisco for twelve years, she lives near the San Bernardino Mountains where she teaches poetry privately. "Snake in the Zendo" appeared in The Burnside Review, and "In the House of Seals" appeared in Terrain.

Julia Vose is the author of *Moved Out on the Inside*, The Figures Press. She is the recipient of NEA grants and Academy of American Poets Prize. "Out of Center, Look Back In" appeared in Ginosko Literary Review, #17.

Laura Walker is the author of *story* (Apogee Press, 2016), *Follow–Haswed* (Apogee Press, 2012), *bird book* (Shearsman Books, 2011), *rimertown/ an atlas* (UC Press, 2008), and *swarm lure* (Battery Press, 2004), and the chapbook *bird book* (Albion Books, 2010). She has taught poetry at San Francisco State University, University of San Francisco, and UC Berkeley Extension. More information can be found at <u>laura-walker. com</u>. Her poems first appeared in *New American Writing*.

Gillian Wegener is the author of the collections *The Opposite of Clairvoyance* (2008) and *This Sweet Haphazard* (2017), both published by Sixteen Rivers Press. She hosts the monthly 2nd Tuesday Reading Series in downtown Modesto, is co-founder of the Modesto-Stanislaus Poetry Center, and served as the poet laureate for the City of Modesto from 2012-2016. "The Opposite of Clairvoyance" was published in *The Oppo-*

site of Clairvoyance, Sixteen Rivers Press, 2008."Road Song, Highway 99" was published in *This Sweet Haphazard*, Sixteen Rivers Press, 2017.

Arisa White's most recent poetry collection is *You're the Most Beautiful Thing that Happened* (Augury Books), nominated for the 29th Lambda Literary Award. She teaches in the low-residency BFA program at Goddard College and is a member of the board of directors for Nomadic Press. arisawhite.com

Toni Wilkes chapbooks *Black Water Beneath a Lid of Ice* and *Stepping Through Moons* received nominations for the California Book Award and the PEN USA Literary Award. A Pushcart Prize and Best of the Net nominee, Wilkes is widely published.

Leonore Wilson taught Creative Writing and English for eighteen years at Napa Valley College and is a former Poet Laurate of Napa. She is on the MFA board of St. Mary's College and the Environmental Literacy Board, as well.

Kathleen Winter's new collection, *I will not kick my friends*, won the 2017 Elixir Poetry Prize and will be published in 2018. New poems are forthcoming in *Yale Review, New Statesman, AGNI, Michigan Quarterly Review, Volt, Prairie Schooner, 32 Poems* and other journals"Glamour" appeared first in *Tin House* ; "Receptive Fields of Single Neurons in the Cat's Striate Cortex" appeared in *American Letters & Commentary*

Pui Ying Wong is the author of two books of poetry, *An Emigrant's Winter* (Glass Lyre Press) and *Yellow Plum Season* (New York Quarterly Books), as well as two chapbooks. Born in Hong Kong, she lives in Cambridge, MA with her husband, the poet Tim Suermondt. "The Flag" was published in the online journal *Up the Staircase.*